WHAT WE SAY
AND **HOW** WE SAY IT

MATTER

ASCD MEMBER BOOK

Many ASCD members received this book as a
member benefit upon its initial release.

Learn more at: **www.ascd.org/memberbooks**

WHAT WE SAY AND **HOW** WE SAY IT

MATTER

Teacher Talk That Improves Student Learning and Behavior

MIKE ANDERSON

Alexandria, Virginia USA

1703 N. Beauregard St. • Alexandria, VA 22311-1714 USA
Phone: 800-933-2723 or 703-578-9600 • Fax: 703-575-5400
Website: www.ascd.org • E-mail: member@ascd.org
Author guidelines: www.ascd.org/write

Ronn Nozoe, *Interim CEO and Executive Director;* Stefani Roth, *Publisher;* Genny Ostertag, *Director, Content Acquisitions;* Julie Houtz, *Director, Book Editing & Production;* Liz Wegner, *Editor;* Judi Connelly, *Associate Art Director;* Jose Coll, *Graphic Designer;* Cynthia Stock, *Typesetter;* Mike Kalyan, *Director, Production Services;* Shajuan Martin, *E-Publishing Specialist;* Kelly Marshall, *Senior Production Specialist*

All web links in this book are correct as of the publication date below but may have become inactive or otherwise modified since that time. If you notice a deactivated or changed link, please e-mail books@ascd.org with the words "Link Update" in the subject line. In your message, please specify the web link, the book title, and the page number on which the link appears.

PAPERBACK ISBN: 978-1-4166-2704-3   ASCD product #119024
PDF E-BOOK ISBN: 978-1-4166-2705-0; see Books in Print for other formats.
Quantity discounts are available: e-mail programteam@ascd.org or call 800-933-2723, ext. 5773, or 703-575-5773. For desk copies, go to www.ascd.org/deskcopy.

ASCD Member Book No. F19-5 (Feb. 2019 P). ASCD Member Books mail to Premium (P), Select (S), and Institutional Plus (I+) members on this schedule: Jan, PSI+; Feb, P; Apr, PSI+; May, P; Jul, PSI+; Aug, P; Sep, PSI+; Nov, PSI+; Dec, P. For current details on membership, see www.ascd.org/membership.

Library of Congress Cataloging-in-Publication Data

Names: Anderson, Mike, 1971– author.
Title: What we say and how we say it matter : teacher talk that improves
    student learning and behavior / Mike Anderson.
Description: Alexandria, Virginia : ASCD, [2019] | Includes bibliographical
    references and index.
Identifiers: LCCN 2018045142 (print) | LCCN 2018058350 (ebook) | ISBN
    9781416627050 (PDF) | ISBN 9781416627043 (pbk.)
Subjects: LCSH: Communication in education. | Teachers—Language. |
    Teacher-student relationships. | Motivation in education. | Effective teaching.
Classification: LCC LB1033.5 (ebook) | LCC LB1033.5 .A54 2019 (print) | DDC
    371.102/2—dc23
LC record available at https://lccn.loc.gov/2018045142

28 27 26 25 24 23 22 21 20 19   2 3 4 5 6 7 8 9 10 11 12

WHAT WE SAY AND HOW WE SAY IT MATTER

What We Say and How We Say It Matter

This is a book about language. More specifically, it's a book about language habits and patterns—the habits and patterns that we use all day and every day in our work with students. We must rely on habits and patterns when it comes to language, for in the midst of all that teachers must do (think ahead about the next step of the activity, keep an eye on the back table of students who seem to be getting off track, keep our other eye on the clock, get reoriented after an announcement blares over the intercom, wonder briefly about the parent who sent an e-mail earlier in the day, notice that three hands just shot up as students seem to be getting confused—and this all in the blink of an eye), there's no way we can consciously think about everything we say before we say it.

Even more specifically, it's a book about the intersection of our language patterns and our best intentions. After all, don't we all have positive intentions and goals for our students? We all want our students to be passionate about learning, to engage in prosocial interactions, to behave positively and appropriately throughout the day—and to do so for the right reasons. For all the discussions and varying opinions about pedagogy in education today, I find that most educators have many of these core values in common. We all want what's best for our students. And yet . . .

We all end up in language patterns that don't match our best intentions. We may even fall into habits that run in direct opposition to what we know is best for our students. Let me illustrate with a story.

At the end of my first year of teaching, I wanted some feedback from my 4th graders, so I created a report card for students to fill out for me and encouraged them to give me honest feedback. It was roughly modeled after the report card our district used for students, though the categories were obviously different. There was a section for comments at the end, and for the most part, the comments were very positive. One, though, caught me off guard. Jenna was a thoughtful and spunky student with whom I thought I shared great rapport. But in her comments, she said something about how I had hurt her feelings sometimes during the year. I was crushed. *Jenna?* I thought. *How could that be? We're always joking around and teasing!* I thanked Jenna for her feedback and asked her to help me understand, apologizing and letting her know I never meant to hurt her feelings. "I know you didn't, Mr. A.," Jenna sighed. "I just couldn't always tell when you were joking and when you were serious." It was a powerful lesson for me—one that I felt like I should have known already. My playful nuanced teasing and joking with 9- and 10-year-olds wasn't always received as intended. I started to pay more careful attention to how I talked with my students, though as you'll see, it took a while for me to shift this habit.

A couple years later, I had the opportunity to work with Paula Denton, who would later author *The Power of Our Words*. She was facilitating a professional development workshop at my school, and she posed a compelling question: "What is a behavior in your class that you find infuriating?" My initial thought was students' overdependence on me. It drove me crazy when students were constantly seeking my approval. "Mr. Anderson, here's my newest poem. Do you like it?" "Mr. A., I just made this new illustration. Do you like it?" "Here's my poster for my project—is it good enough?" During work periods, I sometimes had a line of students waiting to get my approval or waiting to ask me questions that they should have been able to answer on their own.

I found this so infuriating because I wanted my students to be independent. I wanted them to learn to accurately self-assess their work and behavior and feel proud of themselves. I didn't want my students to rely on my opinion but to learn to think for themselves. I also wanted my students to be self-motivated and find inherent satisfaction in their work—not to only feel good about their work if I praised them for it.

Paula pushed us to consider how shifting our language might help alleviate some of the challenging behaviors we saw in our students. I realized that my habit of praising kids using phrases such as "I like the way you . . ." might be a problem. When I wanted to give students positive feedback about their work or behavior, I began with some version of it:

- "Jeremy, I like the way you're working so hard on that math challenge!"
- "Hey, everyone! I loved the way you just walked down the hall so quietly!"
- "Mariceles, I appreciate how much energy you have for this science project!"
- "Ahmad, thank you so much for pushing in your chair after lunch!"

I was, unintentionally, training my students to be teacher-pleasers—to rely on me for their feelings of self-worth or reassurance that they were on the right track. Once I started paying attention to the way I gave students positive feedback, I realized that although I said I believed in a student-centered classroom, my language was awfully teacher-centric. It was out of sync with my beliefs and goals.

I think most of us end up in a place like this with at least some of our language habits. We have the best of intentions. We want our students to feel safe, collaborate well with others, feel ownership for their learning, be joyfully engaged in work, and do the right things for the right reasons. Yet we end up using language patterns that undermine these positive goals. Figure 1.1 illustrates just a few common examples.

FIGURE 1.1

Goals	Conflicting Language Habits
We want students to have ownership of their learning, yet we use language that implies teacher ownership.	• "Some of you still owe me an assignment from last week." • "Here's the next thing you'll do for me." • "You're going to need to show me three key things in this next piece of work."
We want students to feel safe in school and we want to build positive relationships with students, yet we use sarcasm when we get frustrated.	• "Do you think I was put on this planet to clean up your mess?" • "How hard is it to understand the word 'no?'" • "Let's all stop what we're doing and wait for Prince Eli to be ready!"
We want students to view learning as enjoyable, yet we use language that suggests that work stinks.	• "If you finish your work early, you won't have to do any more later." • "I know many of you don't love math, but we've got to get through this unit."
We want students to exhibit good behavior because it's the right thing to do, yet we rely on threats and bribes, implying that they don't want to be good.	• "If you walk quietly in the hallway on our way to music, you'll earn a sticker on our class sticker chart." • "If you're not responsible with your work, you'll have to make up that time later."

So, even more specifically, this is a book about the intersection of our positive intentions and our language habits—and working to better align the two.

Shifting Language to Match New Goals for Students

Where did our bad habits come from, and why is this such a particularly good time to shift them? Many of the most common language habits and patterns have been handed down from teacher to teacher over many years. As new teachers, we look to professional mentors and colleagues for how to speak to children. In teacher preparation programs and internships, we may have been given lots of advice about how to speak with children. We may (consciously or unconsciously) echo our own teachers and parents. What we need to be mindful of, though, is that language patterns that might have worked at one point may not be as effective as they once were. This is the case for a couple of reasons. First, children today are different than children were years ago. I grew up in the tumultuous 1970s and materialistic 1980s—quite a different scene from my parents' experience growing up in the post-World War II 1950s. How could I not have been different from my parents? My two children, who have grown up in the information age, are different from me. Children 20 years from now will be different from children in schools right now. As society, cultural norms, and daily experiences shift, our children change as well. This means that some of our language needs to shift with them.

Perhaps more importantly, especially for educators, our goals for children may change to help them be ready for an ever-changing world. During the industrial age, when public schools came of age, the vast majority of people graduating from schools went on to fairly linear jobs—where they showed up at 9:00, did straightforward work, were managed and motivated by someone else, and then punched out at 5:00. Emphasizing compliance and obedience in schools might have made sense once. This is no longer the case. Skills of creativity, self-motivation, empathy, and collaboration are all more important now than they once were.

Schools also require students to learn higher-level skills than were once expected. When it comes to the social and emotional climate of schools, students no longer spend most of the day working alone doing quiet seat-work. Instead, they need to work together and engage in collaborative tasks with a diverse community of learners. When it comes to academic engagement, it is no longer appropriate for students to be passive recipients of content developed by teachers, textbook publishers, or curricular program companies. Instead, students must assume more power and control of their learning, cocreating rich learning experiences with their teachers. And when it comes to discipline, being obedient rule-followers is no longer enough. Students need to learn to think and act in ethical and responsible ways so they are ready to be independent and deep thinkers, not simply compliant workers.

As I travel the country working with schools in all kinds of settings, I see evidence that these sorts of shifts are happening. Many schools are working at creating more choice-based and project-based learning experiences that emphasize collaboration over competition. Many schools are moving away from traditional grading practices that aim to motivate students through rewards and punishments. And many of these same schools are working at having students play a more active role in discipline by having students create working norms and using restorative justice practices.

However, our teacher talk isn't keeping pace with these new practices, and this sends confusing and counterproductive messages to students. For example, even though teachers may want their students to take more ownership for their work, when they say, "I'm looking for you to turn in a high-quality piece of work," they actually send the message that students are working for teachers. A simple shift such as "Think about what you'll look for in high-quality work" sends a very different message.

Additionally, when you look at the highest-impact practices in education—the ones touted by the top education researchers as having the biggest effect on achievement—language is central to their effectiveness. Consider some of the factors that Marzano (2003) highlights as keys to school and classroom effectiveness and think about the critical role that teacher language plays in each:

- Effective feedback
- Safe and orderly environment
- Collegiality and professionalism
- Classroom management
- Student motivation

Similarly, John Hattie's meta-analysis work (2009), often considered the gold standard in education research, highlights many key practices that yield higher student achievement. The following list is a small sampling of these practices. Again, consider how the language that teachers use will be central to the effectiveness of these practices, all of which rate in the top 26 of the factors Hattie explored. The parenthetical numbers beside each show the effect size on student achievement of the practice. In Hattie's work, an effective size greater than .40 is in the zone of desired effects—practices that yield an above-average impact on achievement.

- Teacher clarity (0.75)
- Feedback (0.73)
- Teacher-student relationships (0.72)
- Metacognitive strategies (0.69)
- Not labeling students (0.61)
- Teaching strategies (0.60)
- Direct instruction (0.59)

Do Changes in Language Really Matter?

Before we begin investing time and energy in reworking our language habits (which is no easy task, trust me), we should first answer a question: Is it worth it? Do changes in language, even small and subtle ones, really make a difference for students? Indeed, there is some compelling evidence that it can make a huge difference.

One of the most famous language shifts studied involves Carol Dweck's research into what she calls mindsets. Dweck shows that when people have a growth mindset, they understand that hard work and effort are the keys to success. Subsequently, they work harder, persist longer, take on more challenging tasks, and achieve at higher levels. When people have a fixed mindset and believe that natural gifts or talents are the basis for success, they tend to shy away from challenges, give up more quickly, and achieve at lower levels. Importantly, in some of the experiments that Dweck and colleagues conducted, very small and subtle language shifts were enough to put children into a fixed or growth mindset. For example, the difference between saying, "Wow, you got [say] eight right. That's a really good score. You must have worked really hard," (after students did well on a nonverbal IQ test) and "Wow, you got [say] eight right. That's a really good score. You must be smart at this," was enough of a difference to put some children (the first example) into a growth mindset and others (the second example) into a fixed one (Dweck, 2006, pp.

71–73). Not only did effort-praised students show more enjoyment of and persistence with harder problems in the next round of tests, but they also outscored their ability-praised peers. Shockingly, when given the chance to share about their scores, 40 percent of ability-praised students said that they got higher scores than they actually received. It may be hard to believe, but one simple language tweak in how students received feedback put students in a completely different emotional state about their learning.

This reminds me of the work of many behavioral economists who highlight how small changes can lead to huge differences in behavior. Want children to make healthier choices in the cafeteria? Place the healthiest foods within easy reach and at eye level. Want more people to save for retirement? Make automatic saving, where money is deducted directly from people's checks, the default so that they have to opt out if they don't want it. Small changes can yield huge results. (If you're interested in exploring this subject in more detail, I highly recommend the work of Richard Thaler and Cass Sunstein, including their book *Nudge*. You might also look to Steven Levitt and Stephen Dubner of *Freakonomics* fame.)

Again, consider the effect of small changes in language. If the subtle shift from "you must be so smart" to "you must have worked hard" can have such a profound influence on students' learning, consider other potential changes and their benefits. If we want students to be independent and self-motivated, we might replace "I love the way you're solving that problem so creatively" (emphasizing teacher approval) with "You're working to solve that problem with such creativity" (emphasizing student work). If we want students to grow into more ethical and moral thinkers, we might replace "Walk quietly in the halls and we'll get a sticker on our sticker chart" with "Walking quietly in the halls helps us take care of learners in other classrooms."

A Few Important Points Before We Continue

The rest of this book digs into various language habits and patterns, and the goal with each is to bring our language closer to our best intentions and the positive goals we have for students. First, let's consider a few more points.

We're All Teachers

Throughout this book, the word "teacher" is used in a broad and inclusive way. Whether you are a classroom teacher, unified arts specialist, special education tutor, principal, superintendent, office assistant, custodian, paraprofessional, or parent, you are a teacher. Anyone who has a role to play in the lives of children fits the bill. Throughout this book, please consider "teacher" to be a broad and inclusive term.

All Teachers Have a Different Voice—and That's Okay

In the chapters that follow, you'll see many suggestions for language examples. There are many "Instead of, Try This" charts, which offer starting points for language to use. You'll need to take the spirit of these suggestions and starting points and adapt them so they feel like you. We all have our own unique voices and personalities, and we shouldn't all try and use the exact same language. One of the most demeaning trends in education in the past decade or so has been the proliferation of boxed curricula that script teacher language in lessons. While suggestions for what to say (and how to say it) can be helpful, we shouldn't try to create teacher-bots who offer pat automatic responses or phrases in any given situation. So, if you decide to move away from "I like the way you . . ." when giving positive feedback, consider many alternatives and find ones that work for you.

It's Not Just What We Say, It's How We Say It

It's almost impossible to separate tone from the actual words we say, and tone is something that can be hard to convey in a book. So, in each chapter—with each language habit we explore together—be mindful of the goals of the language and consider how tone will influence the messages students receive. A slight change in intonation—a subtle shift in a smile or eye contact—can dramatically change how language feels for students. A playful roll of the eyes, a shake of the head, and an upturn in our voice that accompanies a comment ("Oh, Anna! How do you ever find anything in that desk?!") may help us build a connection with a student. That same language delivered with a disappointed tone, a scowl, and an admonishing finger conveys a much different message.

Consider, for example, the many different messages we can convey with the phrase "Excuse me." We might say "Excuse me" when we bump into a student accidentally. Used with a quiet voice and apologetic tone, this phrase expresses remorse. This phrase means something quite different if we're asking someone to repeat something they said because we didn't hear or understand them. "Excuse me?" we ask with a curious and interested tone. Both of these feel respectful and appropriate, but we all know that this same phrase can have more negative meanings. If the first word is emphasized with a raised voice ("*Excuse* me!"), it is now an attempt to get the attention of the class, and it feels a bit sharp. With an angry, lowered voice and eyebrows raised, "Excuse me?" feels ominous and threatening.

This is important to keep in mind, and we'll return to this idea often throughout the book. It's not just what we say that matters, it's how we say it.

We're Always Modeling

In one school where I taught, there was a K–5 strand of teachers who formed a school within a school. Most students moved through this "constellation" from kindergarten through 5th grade. I'll never forget Ruth Ann, the 3rd grade teacher in this constellation, commenting on how her students sounded so positive and polite at the beginning of each year, having spent an entire 2nd grade together in Gary's classroom: "It's wonderful. Each year, 25 little Garys walk through my door on the first day of school!" I'll also never forget the years in another school when I inherited 5th graders from 4th grade teachers who used sneering sarcasm on a daily basis. It would take months to break students of their habits of insulting each other and laughing at each other as they made mistakes.

In several places in this book, teacher modeling is addressed specifically, but in some ways, this entire book is about modeling. A wise mentor once told me, "Kids are always watching us. Little people watch big people to figure out how to become big people." We should always keep this in mind.

All day long, we are the tone-setters for students and model what grown-up behavior should look and sound like. How do we talk about work and learning? How do we deal with frustration and anger? What kinds of words are appropriate in a school setting? How do we interact with a student who is struggling? In any given situation, the way we talk and act gives students important clues and signals about how they themselves should act as well. This is one of the golden opportunities of teaching—that we get to help students grow into kind, compassionate, thoughtful, people. So, let's work at using the language that we want our students to use.

Allow Yourself to Be Uncomfortable

It can be hard for us to be in a place of learning when it comes to language because language is so central to everything we do. We want definitive answers about what we should say, and we want them now. This can lead us to one of two shortcuts when it comes to language change, both of which I'd like to discourage. The first is unquestioning compliance—a ready acceptance of what someone says because they happen to be at the front of the room teaching a workshop or because they wrote a book about the topic. "Just tell me what to say!" I've heard some educators beg. Or, "Last year a trainer told us to call out the good behavior of some children to get the others to follow, and now you're saying we shouldn't do that?!" Good language habits require intentional thought, so please don't simply jump to new patterns too quickly.

For most of us, teaching isn't just a job, it's our identity. We *are* teachers. This makes examining our practice more than just an exercise in skills or strategies—it can feel like soul searching or even therapy, which can be scary. This can lead us to a second shortcut: quickly dismissing a language suggestion and not thinking about it at all. "Well, sarcasm works in my classroom. My kids like it," is a comment I've heard more than once. Like blind compliance, quick dismissiveness takes us out of the action. It disengages us, making it impossible to learn and grow.

This book is meant to push your thinking and encourage deep reflection and rich discussions with colleagues. In the end, you will need to decide what language habits you should work on. You'll need to consider your positive goals for students and decide what language will best help you get there. I hope that the many suggestions in this book will support you in this journey.

2

Show Respect for All Students

What do students most value in teachers? It's a powerful and important question, and I've asked it of dozens of students in many schools. The way I ask the question varies by grade. In primary grades, I might ask, "What do you like about teachers?" In middle elementary grades it might sound like, "What do you wish all teachers were like?" With middle and high school students, I might ask, "What do you wish all teachers believed about students and learning?" Responses vary widely, but themes emerge, and the most common theme that I see is one of respect. Students want to be treated fairly and with dignity. Here are a few excerpts from interviews I've conducted with students:

1st grader: All teachers should believe that kids are really nice. If teachers didn't like kids, school would be nothing.

4th grader: I would have to say . . . well, my first initial thought was no homework . . . but, then, what I really want is for teachers to kind of have more higher expectations for kids and for them to have more responsibility, and I would like if the teachers could let us, you know, do more things that like say the 6th graders would do because I think that we deserve more of the responsibility because we're getting pretty old now, and I would like if I could be treated as though I were like an adult or another teacher.

8th grader: Students are capable of both logical and abstract thought—we come to more conclusions than they (teachers) think we do. We see deeper into things than sometimes teachers think.

9th grader: Almost like they're equal with kids. Like they're not just here as a teacher but here as a friend. Not like I'm here, I'm teaching you this, blah, blah, blah. Or like "I control you." More like being on a level standing with the kids. So that kids felt more open to ask questions. Like I know personally I'm not going to ask a teacher a question if all I get from them is a "What do you want?" or "What do you need help with now?" That kind of thing.

My informal student survey results align with more thorough research done on this subject. John Hattie's work is once again helpful. In *Visible Learning and the Science of How We Learn* (2014), he and cognitive scientist Gregory Yates pose an important question: Can your students trust you? They answer: "It is crucial to be able to manage a successful learning environment, which, in itself, entails your exhibiting attributes that promote positive and open human communication. Students value being treated with (a) fairness, (b) dignity, and (c) individual respect. These threefold aspects have emerged strongly in all studies in which students are interviewed and surveyed as to what they expect of their teachers" (p. 26).

It's important to recognize that this represents a dramatic shift from "children should be seen but not heard" and "spare the rod and spoil the child." In previous generations, much of the emphasis of child-rearing seemed to be on minimizing children's sense of power. Adult authority was about having power over children—"keeping children in their place"—as opposed to empowering them.

What we must be mindful of, then, is how our language may help or hinder these efforts. We must examine our habits with an eye toward students' sense of power. Does our language support students' developing sense of positive identity? Does it help students feel a sense of empowerment and agency? Or, might some of our language patterns do the reverse—make students feel less powerful, smaller, weaker?

Teasing Gone Wrong

Remember when students filled out a report card for me and 4th grader Jenna gave me some powerful feedback about my use of teasing? Here's another time when it went poorly. (What can I say, it took me a while to shift this habit. In fact, I'm still working on it.) Stacy stalked into the classroom, a thundercloud hovering over her head. She snapped at a friend as she entered and gave me a short response when I said "Good morning." A bit stung perhaps, I responded, "Well! Aren't you just a bowl of peaches this morning?" Tears immediately welled in her eyes, and she lashed out, "I'm having a bad morning, okay! Just leave me alone!"

This is the danger of teasing. When misplaced or misused, it can backfire and make a bad situation worse. Stacy already knew she was grumpy and didn't need my snarky comment to point it out publicly. Though I might easily defend my teasing (*but Stacy and I have great rapport, and I was just trying to lighten the mood*), it was a bad call.

Early in my career, teasing was one language habit that I forced myself to examine. Though there were times when playful teasing did help build rapport and strengthen relationships with students, there were other times that it didn't work as I intended. When I meant it to scold, teach a lesson, or highlight a flaw, it nearly always was the wrong call—feeling disrespectful of students at times when they were already feeling badly.

Sarcasm—to Tear Flesh

Invariably, when I talk with teachers about the use of language in classrooms, especially at the middle and high school level, the topic of sarcasm surfaces. Some are quick to defend its use: "But my students are old enough to get sarcasm." Others contend, "My students love sarcasm. They use it all the time themselves. Teenagers are sarcastic by nature. Every time I use it, the class laughs." This all may be true. Older students may be more capable of understanding and may be more likely to use sarcasm, but that hardly justifies its use. After all, true sarcasm is meant to hurt. The Merriam-Webster dictionary defines sarcasm as "a sharp and often satirical or ironic utterance designed to cut or give pain" and notes that its Greek word of origin, *sarkazein,* meant "to tear flesh like a dog" (*Merriam-Webster Online,* n.d.).

Sarcasm in the classroom almost certainly stunts learning. In a fascinating exploration of body language, former FBI agent Joe Navarro names sarcasm as a form of aggression and warns against its use: "Aggressive tactics can lead to emotional turmoil, making it difficult to concentrate and think clearly . . . our cognitive abilities are hijacked so that the limbic brain can have full use of all available cerebral resources" (2008, p. 34). In fact, if we understand that using sarcasm with students is a form of exerting power over them (would you allow your students to use biting sarcasm with you?), it almost certainly constitutes bullying—"a behavior by a person or group that establishes, asserts, or maintains social power over another person and causes pain or humiliation" (Crowe, 2012, p. 3). Sarcasm creates a stressful learning environment, and neuroimaging research reveals that brains over-stimulated by stress are less able to learn (Willis, 2006, pp. 24–25).

Now, before you beat yourself up as you worry about the amount of sarcasm you use, we should reassess what sarcasm is actually all about. This is a term that is often overgeneralized. As I've spoken with teachers, I've heard many talk about sarcasm a bit too broadly, using it to describe many different types of language, some of which may also be damaging while others may not. Examine the examples below to think about this some more.

- "Well! It's another beautiful day out there!" (It's raining, and it has been for days.) This statement is ironic, not sarcastic. The teacher says one thing and means another, but the comment is not directed at a student and is not mean-spirited. Students with language processing challenges or students who are learning English might be confused by the twist of meaning, but there is probably no real harm done here to a sense of community. Still, if irony is used too often—if the general tone of the teacher is ironic—the spirit of the class can start to wither.

- As a teacher jots a few notes on the board, he says, "Oh boy. Here I go again. You all know that I can't spell to save my life. Does anyone remember how to spell 'Bernoulli?'" This is self-deprecation, not sarcasm. In Chapter 12 we'll consider challenges and potential pitfalls of overusing self-deprecation. For our exploration here, I think it's safe to say that it doesn't diminish students' sense of self or create a combative or corrosive classroom community.

- Corey is staring out the window instead of writing. His teacher says, "Corey, I love how hard you're working!" Said with a positive and light tone—the intention might be to remind Corey of what he should be doing—this kind of false flattery is confusing. Said with a wry or ironic tone, it's clearly sarcastic and meant to hurt. Instead, his teacher should just remind: "Corey, refocus on your work."

- "Thanks so much for that thoughtful response" (in a tone that clearly indicates that the teacher thinks the response was a poor one). This is sarcasm, and it's demeaning. Students may chuckle at this retort by the teacher, but this laughter likely means one of two things. Either students are joining in the ridiculing of a classmate, or they are nervous and hope the next mean comment isn't directed at them. Comments like this create a climate of fear and mean-spiritedness.

> **Reassess Environmental Print**
>
> Though not verbal, environmental print is part of the language of the classroom—teacher talk that surrounds students and influences the tone of the room. Watch out for "Stop global whining" or "This is a no whining zone" posters. Though whining might drive us crazy, hanging these kinds of signs in our rooms displays a low expectation of students. There's also a negative and sharp tone to these kinds of displays—they're like little sarcastic beacons that blink nonstop in our classrooms. Take them down.

- "What part of, 'Sit down and listen' did you not understand?" This may or may not be sarcasm. Even with a light tone it likely sounds snarky. With a caustic tone it is certainly mean-spirited. Instead, be direct and remind students: "Remember, it's time to sit down and listen."
- "You're 12 years old! You should know better than to doodle on a desk!" This isn't sarcasm, but it is a form of shaming. By implying that a student is acting younger than he or she should, we likely evoke anxiety and guilt. Instead, we might just hand the child a sponge.

We could go on and on with examples, but I think this is enough to drive home the point. When the effect of language is to "knock students down a peg," we are reducing their chances of engaging in powerful learning. Figure 2.1 offers some alternatives to sarcastic comments.

FIGURE 2.1	
Instead of . . .	**Try This . . .**
"Excuse me, Michael? Do you think you're the only person in this class? There are other students who need my attention too!"	"Michael, I'll get to you in a moment. I have a few other students to touch base with, and then I'll come see you."
"Oh, what a surprise, Lisa. You didn't bring in your homework again. Are you going for some kind of record or something?"	"You're having a hard time bring in homework, Lisa. Let's sit down later and see if we can come up with some ideas to help you out."
"Do I look like a maid? Do you think I was put on this planet to clean up your mess?"	"Q'von, remember to clean up your snack wrapper."

Drop Labels

It can be so easy to think of students in categories. We have boys and girls in our classrooms. Some students are white, some are Asian, some are Latino, some are black. Some kids like music, and others like sports. Our brains seem to be wired to categorize—to sort things (and people) into groups and categories—to make sense and order out of overwhelming variability. We probably aren't even aware that we're doing so. The problem with this is that labels can narrow how we see our children.

Instead, we can probably drop the labels and group names all together. A teacher might mean to be inclusive while saying, "We're all going to work as a team—whether you're a jock, a bookworm, an artist, or a math geek." Instead of feeling included however, students are likely trying to figure out which group they belong to. *I'm on the soccer team, but I like to read. Am I jock or a bookworm?* a student might wonder. The teacher didn't say, and probably doesn't believe, that you can't be both, but it was implied. Regardless, these kinds of messages may reduce students' overall sense of power, as they feel confined to the boxes in which they are placed, as well as encourage students to see each other in terms of categories and cliques.

Be Aware of Implicit Bias (and Fight Against It)

I'll never forget hearing anti-racism activist Jane Elliott speak at Connecticut College when I was an undergraduate student. Bright-eyed and brimming with a sense of social justice, I was eager to have my vision of myself as a thoughtful, considerate, accepting person reinforced by the famous teacher who confronted racism in her 3rd grade class through the now legendary Blue Eyes/Brown Eyes exercise. Jane strode onto the stage and faced all of us squarely. She began her talk by pointing at all of us in the audience and announcing, "You are all prejudiced." I recoiled. *No, I'm not! I have friends who are black!* I naively thought. Jane then went on to explain that we all (herself included) have biases and prejudices and that we must constantly work at bringing these to the surface so we can examine them. That's the only way we'll be able to get rid of them.

None of us wants to think of ourselves as biased. We all want to believe that race, gender, sexuality, socioeconomic status, and other factors don't play a role in how we speak to or about our students. And yet, as Sarah Fiarman explains in her fantastic article, "Unconscious Bias: When Good

Intentions Aren't Enough" (2016), we all harbor unconscious biases, and "these biases influence us even when they are in direct opposition to our espoused beliefs—and sometimes in opposition to our own lived experience."

Here's an example. A well-intentioned music teacher is addressing the 5th grade chorus, announcing the songs that would be sung at the winter concert. She begins by listing several traditional Christmas songs and then concludes, "And for our Jewish friends, we're going to sing a special Hanukkah song." While meaning to be inclusive of students who were Jewish, it sends the reverse message. The teacher is clearly talking to everyone else, and the Jewish students are on the outside looking in.

Watch Our Responses and Reactions

I had a moment recently when I recognized an implicit bias I had—when an unconscious bias became conscious. My family and I had driven to Montreal for a short trip during a school vacation week. I wasn't surprised to see a wide ethnic diversity as we walked the downtown streets, but I did realize that it came as a surprise to me when I heard people of Asian, Middle Eastern, and African descent speaking French. Of course, in a French-speaking city, it makes sense to expect people in the city to speak French, but having grown up in a community in Maine where the only people who I knew who spoke French were white, I was surprised. I'm a little embarrassed to admit this, but it highlights that we probably all harbor biases, and we need to work at making them conscious so we can control our responses and reactions in the short term and retrain ourselves in the long term.

Imagine the messages we might send (and the biases we might continue to perpetuate) through our daily interactions with students. A 6th grade boy comes up to us and shares a quilt he's been working on at home. "You quilt?" we exclaim in surprise. "Do kids tease you because of that?" Even if we ask these questions with a positive and interested voice, we've accidentally reinforced the idea that it's unusual for a boy to sew. Instead, we might simply ask some questions about his work. "What has been fun or challenging about this project?" "How much bigger do you plan on making it?" "Are you making it for yourself or is it a gift for someone?"

In his powerful article "Let's Talk About Racism in Schools" (2016), educator Rick Wormeli encourages us to recognize and control micro-aggressions, "the small, seemingly nonracist things people do, say, and think that are hurtful and may betray unconscious racism or bias. Examples include: avoiding eye contact with students outside our culture; telling a student her math work is excellent for a student who comes from such a poor background; demeaning service industry jobs or any job perceived as being done primarily by minorities ("If you don't study, you might wind up as a taxi driver"); and using language like saying black youths "rioted and turned violent," whereas white youths "protested unfair treatment."

Respectful Language Is Especially Important with Students Who Struggle

When students are treated with dignity and respect, they are readier to learn. And this is crucial for *all* students. This is important to highlight because it's pretty easy to be respectful and humane with children who come to school with strong social and emotional skills, display kindness, and follow rules. Unfortunately, the students who come to us in most desperate need of daily doses of respect, empathy, and compassion are the very ones it can be hardest to treat kindly. We might worry that being respectful to kids who are being belligerent or rude would somehow reinforce their negative behavior. "Once they can treat me with respect, they'll get it in return," we might rationalize. Instead, this is more like withholding an inhaler from someone suffering an asthma attack, reasoning, "Once they can breathe properly, they'll deserve their inhaler."

Let's keep this in mind as we consider using respectful language with students. How will children who themselves struggle with respectful behavior ever learn how to behave appropriately if they don't receive lots of respect?

Conclusion

Once again, we should consider our best intentions and positive goals for students. If we want students to act with self-confidence, feel strong enough to take charge of their own learning, and learn to exhibit respect for others, we must consider our own language. Which of our habits will support these goals, and which ones might undermine them? By exhibiting respect for all students, we can help student grow into strong and respectful people.

3

Create a Culture of Collaboration

As students spend more and more time working together, it is essential for teachers to create classroom climates that are conducive to collaboration. This certainly wasn't always the case. In fact, for a long time in schools, the reverse was true. Solo seatwork was the norm, and students rarely worked together. Teachers passed out tests in order of grades from highest to lowest, hoping that the fear of doing worse than classmates (or the prospect of beating them) would inspire students to work harder. Bell curves and scaled test scores meant that academic success was more about how students ranked among their classmates than it was about how well they understood content. Science fairs and spelling bees publicly pitted students against each other, and all students were required to participate.

I remember how negative and combative the climate was when I was in high school classes where tests were scaled. I'd get my test back and see something like a 78 written at the top. I'd immediately look to my classmates who almost always scored at the top of the class, praying that they got a low grade. After all, if the top score was an 85, we'd all get a 15-point bonus and my score would shoot from a 78 to a 93—the difference between a C and an A! If they got a high score, they could count on getting angry glares and comments from others (myself included, I'm embarrassed to say). "Jason! C'mon!" we'd grump. "Danielle! What the heck!"

While some of these competitive practices are still used in schools, they are slowly fading as a new paradigm emerges. Schools are moving away from comparative grading practices toward competency and skill-based assessments. Students are engaging with each other more often through partner chats, team challenges, and complex integrated long-range group project work.

Some may question whether this shift is good for students. After all, aren't students entering a dog-eat-dog competitive world after school? In fact, skills of collaboration and teamwork are highly valued in the workplace. In a survey of business leaders conducted by Northeastern University (2014), communication and interpersonal skills were two of the top five most desired skills that employers are looking for in employees. In a report published by the Center on Education Policy (Frizzell, Braun, Ferguson, Rentner, & Kober, 2017), working collaboratively and communication skills are listed as two of the key "deeper learning competencies" needed for career readiness. The report is based on a detailed analysis of data from more than 900 jobs and careers and indicates that these skills will be increasingly important in the more complex jobs of the coming years. This matches a conversation I recently had with a professor of engineering at the University of New Hampshire. He related that their business advisory team—a group of local engineers who help them understand what UNH grads will need to thrive in the workplace—keeps emphasizing the need for students to have skills of collaboration so they can work well with others effectively as engineers.

Effective communication and collaboration are the very skills that are less likely to be outsourced or automated as our economy continues to shift away from the industrial age and into the information age. Being able to collaborate effectively will enable students to weather the radical changes underway in our economy.

Creating classroom atmospheres where students see each other as collaborators as opposed to competitors (it's hard to be both) is clearly something to strive for. However, even as we shift other practices in schools, we may find that we continue to use language that encourages competition over collaboration.

Reduce Judgmental and Comparative Language

Have you ever said to a group, perhaps in a class discussion, "Who has a great idea to share?" We probably all have. *And what's wrong with that?* you might wonder. Though you might have used the word "great" to inspire students or to set a positive tone for the discussion, that word might be problematic. It encourages students to compare themselves to others. Some students might hesitate to share, wondering if their idea qualifies as great. Others might view the sharing of ideas as a competition to see who can share the best idea.

Comparative or judgmental words slide into our daily talk so easily. This language is even promoted in some literacy programs and approaches that encourage teachers to use the term "good readers" and "good writers" when describing reading strategies. ("Good writers don't fall in love with a first draft—they know they'll need to go back and revise." "Good readers use context clues to figure out words they don't know.") The intention of this language is positive. We want students to be good readers and writers and aspire to be good readers and writers. So, what's the problem? First of all, students already want to be good readers and writers, don't they? Why would any student not want to be a good reader or writer? Second, when we use judgmental language, we may move students away from thinking about the reading or writing strategy and into self-judgment mode. *Am I a good writer? I don't like to revise, so does that mean that I'm a bad writer?* We may even provoke a twinge of anxiety. *If I can't revise well yet, does that mean I'm not a good writer?* Or, *Does it mean that I'm not good as Lisa, who is really good at revising?*

Clearly, not all students are going to have these reactions, and even the ones who do may not be conscious of them. Still, these small moments build up and can contribute to a classroom atmosphere that feels judgmental or comparative—conditions that make it harder for students to take the risks necessary for learning.

So, what might we say instead? When possible, simply remove judgmental or comparative words such as "good," "great," "best," "worst," and "awesome." Instead of saying, "Who has a cool idea to share with the class?"

simply ask, "Who has an idea to share with the class?" or emphasize why a strategy or technique might be helpful in neutral terms. Instead of having students compare themselves to each other, help them practice skills of self-reflection (see Figure 3.1).

FIGURE 3.1

Instead of . . .	Try This . . .
"Who has a great idea to share?"	"Who has an idea to share?"
"Good readers use context clues to figure out new words."	"Using context clues can help you figure out new words."
"Raise your hand if you finished at least five problems. How many of you finished 10? How about more than 10?"	"Turn and talk with a partner. What was a strategy you used to help you stay focused during our work period today?"
"Some of you did really well on this quiz, and some of you didn't. I think some of you need to study a bit more."	"Once you look at your quiz, turn it over and jot down the study strategies you tried. On a scale of 1 to 5, rate how effective you think the strategy was for you."
"Good mathematicians think about multiple pathways to a solution."	"Thinking about multiple pathways to a solution helps you better understand mathematical concepts."

Avoid Manipulative Praise

Two students are supposed to be cleaning up after an activity. Jackson is picking up, and Malia is still playing with some of the materials. The teacher walks over and, while glancing at Malia, says, "I love the way Jackson is cleaning up his materials!" In this case, the teacher isn't really talking to Jackson, he's talking to Malia. He's using the good behavior of one student to manipulate another.

This is a classic teacher management strategy that continues to be taught in many teacher preparation programs and classroom management workshops. I used it myself for many years, and it seemed to work, at least in the short term. Almost always, Malia will get the idea and get back on track. While this management strategy may fix the problem in the moment, we should consider the potential longer-term negative consequences. We're using the good behavior of Jackson to manipulate the behavior of Malia. In a sense, we're using a form of manipulation that can be confusing and even passive aggressive. Though it may seem gentler to praise Jackson's good behavior instead of redirecting Malia, we put both students in an awkward social situation. Malia is now supposed to imitate Jackson, which can lead to resentment. Jackson is put up as the model for Malia, which can feel awkward and embarrassing. Without meaning to, we are saying to these students that they are in competition with each other, and Jackson is winning. Consider how you might feel if an administrator did this to you in a staff meeting ("I like the way Jeannie is staying focused and not having side conversations right now!"). This is a language habit that we must collectively reconsider as a profession.

Instead, let's be direct and sincere. We should give a brief and simple reminder. "Malia, remember, it's time to clean up." If we want to acknowledge Jackson's behavior, we should do so quietly and on the side. "Jackson, the way you're cleaning up is helping us get ready for our next activity!" See Figure 3.2 for more examples.

FIGURE 3.2		
Situation	**Instead of . . .**	**Try This . . .**
Brian is wandering around the classroom. Joe is settling in and getting to work.	"Brian! Look at how nicely Joe is getting to work!"	"Brian, it's time to settle in to work."
Some students are sitting quietly, ready for a mini-lesson. Others are chatting instead of listening.	"I love how Mariah, Tarique, and Rachel are all sitting quietly and ready to go."	(First, use a signal to get the attention of the group.) "I'm about to give a quick lesson. It's time to listen."
The class is playing math games in cooperative groups. Several groups are focused, and a few aren't.	"I like how Michaela's, Bobby's, and Devan's groups are focused on their math games."	(Go to groups who are unfocused.) "Hey, everyone. It's time to get focused on the math game."

If we still want to use the positive behavior of some to help get others back on track, we can do so in general terms: "It looks like about half of the class has remembered to get their writers notebook for today's quick write." This allows us to use the positive behavior of some students as a reminder without putting individual students on the spot.

Conclusion

Chances are, if we use language that encourages competition over collaboration, we're hoping to inspire and motivate students to participate, put in great effort, and do great work. More specifically, we're probably hoping to inspire and motivate certain students—ones who may shy away from participation or lack motivation and effort. Though our intentions are good, we're likely *demotivating* these very students. Further, these language habits do little harm to students who are already engaged and successful. In fact, they likely reinforce their sense of success and superiority. But the very students who most need a safe and neutral playing field to take the risks needed for learning may further retreat and be less likely to invest energy and emotion into a losing proposition.

Additionally, we shouldn't be fooled by the students who seem to thrive on competition. You know the ones I mean—students who are constantly comparing themselves to others. They're the ones who shout out, "I'm finished!" as they complete an assignment. They likely ask other kids what grades they got on tests or

> ### Other Strategies for Building a Culture of Collaboration
>
> - Make sure all students learn and use each other's names.
> - Create class rules together based on students' academic and social goals.
> - Work on class academic projects such as creating instructional videos, a class anthology of writing, or a class bulletin board.
> - Build student relationships through fun activities and lots of partner or group work.
> - Use flexible seating so students learn to work with a variety of peers.

papers, hoping to show that their score was higher. Their behavior often presents as bragging, and it's important to recognize that this isn't a result of confidence or joy but a lack of it. Students who feel self-confident and secure don't need to compare themselves to others to feel validated about their work. Let's deemphasize comparison in the classroom to allow all students to feel a sense of accomplishment and self-worth.

4

Develop Students' Positive Identity

Do you want your students to be strong and confident or retiring and meek? Do you want students to feel confident enough to ask questions when they're confused? Do you want students to act with what Peter Johnston calls "agency"—an understanding that if they act strategically, they can accomplish their goals (2004, p. 29)? I think we all want students who can act with initiative and take on the challenges of powerful learning. In *Embarrassment: And the Emotional Underlife of Learning*, Tom Newkirk (2017) makes the powerful argument that this kind of learning requires a state of vulnerability—it requires learners to be in a place where they may make a mistake or be unsuccessful. People tend to be risk-averse and avoid these kinds of situations; the risk of embarrassment outweighs the potential positive outcomes of being right or learning. Thus, it takes an inner fortitude to place oneself in this position. Students must feel a sense of inner strength and resiliency to be a true learner.

You want your students to feel confident enough to try new things, strong enough to ask for help, and to generally have a positive sense of self. One of the most basic ways we can support this is through the way we address our students. So, here's the driving question of this chapter: How can we name students in ways that support these goals?

The Power of Names

Have you read the *Earthsea Trilogy* by Ursula K. LeGuin? The series is not as well-known as *The Chronicles of Narnia* or *The Lord of the Rings*, but it's every bit as rich and powerful. In these stories, names are the source of all power and sorcery. It is by knowing something (or someone's) true name that wizards derive their powers. In *A Wizard of Earthsea* (1968), LeGuin explains: "No one knows a man's true name but himself and his namer. He may choose at length to tell it to his brother, or his wife, or his friend, yet even those few will never use it where any third person may hear it.... Who knows a man's name, holds that man's life in his keeping" (p. 69). She elaborates in *The Tombs of Autuan* (1970): "To weave the magic of a thing, you see, one must find its true name. In my lands we keep our true names hidden all our lives long, from all but those whom we trust utterly; for there is great power, and great peril, in a name" (p. 107).

Names are a part of who we are. They give us a sense of self-worth and power. The simple habit of using students' names helps them feel known and valued. Let's explore some of the ways we might name students and consider how these patterns might affect how they feel.

Use Students' Real or Preferred Names

At the beginning of the year, it's critical that we learn and practice using students' real names—the names they want to be called in school. This shows that we value who they are and that they are important. This is a habit to practice right away. The further we get into a school year without knowing our students' names, the more awkward and disrespectful the situation becomes. A colleague of mine was visiting a school and observing in a 5th grade classroom. She noticed that the teacher was in the habit of addressing students using "ma'am" and "sir." After speaking with the teacher about this, she was horrified to find that the teacher didn't know many of the names of the students in her room. It was November! Sadly, this isn't as uncommon as we would like to think. Having shared this story with many, I have often heard the response, "Oh, I know someone who doesn't know all of their students' names." This is quite simply unprofessional and disrespectful.

In addition to the basic practice of learning students' names, we should make sure we know the names that students prefer to be called in school. You may find that students have a preferred name that's different than their given one. Though my immediate family (parents, sister, grandparents) has always called me "Michael," to everyone else, I am "Mike." It felt uncomfortable, almost too intimate, when someone at school called me "Michael." One year, one of my students named Charles preferred to be called "Charlie," but the next year (we looped together from 4th to 5th grade) he wanted to be called "Chuck." It took me quite a while to adjust to this new name!

> **Strategies for Learning Names**
>
> - Have students wear name tags for the first two weeks of school.
> - Use students' names as often as possible early in the year.
> - Practice remembering students' names in your head during your commute.
> - Encourage students to use each other's names in class. The more often names are used, the better!

At the same time, we want to make sure that the names students want us to call them are genuine and appropriate. Names that are silly should also be avoided. One year on the first day of school I was checking on students' preferred names as I made name tags for take-home folders. I asked Dylan, "You prefer 'Dylan,' right?" I saw his eyes twinkle as he glanced quickly at a friend. "Call me Bob," he said. I gave him a quick playful wink and said, "I'll put down 'Dylan' for now, and we can chat later." When I touched base later, he admitted that he was just kidding around and that everyone called him Dylan.

We also must be careful not to assume. A colleague of mine told me how, at the beginning of one school year, he refused to call a student by his preferred name, Bubba, changing it to his given name of Alex. He was soon visited by the boy's parents who straightened him out: Bubba was a family name passed down through several generations, and it was what everyone called "Alex." "Boy did I feel like a knucklehead," remarked my friend. Though he had the best of intentions, it was a valuable lesson learned!

We must also pay attention to pronunciation. It has been shown that students can be negatively affected by teachers' failure to pronounce their names correctly (Kohli & Solorzano, 2012). Especially when students come from backgrounds that are different from yours, you may be unfamiliar with the correct pronunciation of some names, so it is up to you to learn them. You might need to ask students multiple times, "Did I pronounce your name correctly?" And if not, have them teach you. Practice right away. I've had some students try and dismiss this with a "Don't worry, Mr. Anderson. That's close enough," but I insist. "Nope. Close enough won't cut it. I need to make sure I'm getting this right."

Are Nicknames Okay?

You may wonder—are nicknames okay? After all, nicknames aren't students' real names, but don't they build rapport or set a tone of playfulness and comradery?

It depends.

On one hand, nicknames can be playful and fun, and they can show a special bond between teacher and student. On the other hand, what does it say if some students have nicknames and others don't? I've been guilty of this as a classroom teacher—having playful names for some students but not others. That's a language habit I shifted once I realized that by valuing some, I may have been diminishing the value and respect felt by others. My suggestion is that if you're going to have playful nicknames for some students, you should have them for all.

What About Terms of Endearment?

Many teachers use terms of endearment when addressing their students. It is perhaps one of the most common language patterns that I see in schools, especially at the elementary level. "Honey," "sweetie," and especially the more recent "kiddo" are intended to build trust and show affection, but they may feel patronizing or condescending. I once spoke with a 7th grader who hated when his teacher called him "sweetie." He knew she meant well, and he never asked her to stop (imagine how hard that would be to do as a student!), but it was clear that he felt devalued, and it rankled him.

You may be wondering, but isn't teaching also about nurturing? When teachers use terms like "sweetie" and "honey," aren't they building rapport and setting a tone of caring? That's certainly the intent. I've never met a teacher who used terms of endearment to make children feel submissive. And yes, part of our job is to be nurturing and caring. A challenge, then, is to consider other ways of being caring and nurturing while also empowering students. For example, we can kneel down so we're at the eye level of young children as we talk with them. We can use warm and supportive body language, facial expressions, and tones of voice to send messages of authentic caring and concern. We can show genuine interest in what they're doing, asking them interesting and interested questions. These kinds of practices exude warmth and caregiving without belittling students.

En Francais? En Español?

What about the world language practice of having students have different names during language class? I sat down and talked with Barbara Milliken who teaches French and Spanish at Oyster River High School in Durham, New Hampshire. She explained the rationale behind having students choose and adopt a different name in a world language class. (My son Ethan is "Dominique" in French class, and my daughter Carly is "Ana" in Spanish class.) Barbara explained that learning a language requires students to take frequent risks—trying to speak a new language is hard and scary at any time of life, let alone during adolescence when public mistakes can be especially humiliating. By taking on a new name, students get to, in a sense, take on a different persona during foreign language class.

Additionally, when students get to create their world language name, they can feel empowered, which is important when learning a new language. This can help them actually *be someone else* as they work at learning a new language. It might be easier to take a chance on pronouncing a new word as Dominique or Ana.

As you consider using nicknames with students, it is important to ask yourself, what is my goal? Why are you using nicknames? Will the use of nicknames help or hurt students' sense of self and feeling of inclusion and safety in the room? Will the names help them feel a sense of power and agency, or will they diminish this, making them feel lesser—lower than others?

Use Names Positively

We should also consider how children hear their name used throughout the day. While some children hear their names used primarily in a positive context ("Mary! How was your weekend?" "Markus, thanks so much for helping set up art materials this morning!"), other children, may end up hearing their names used negatively over and over again ("Silas! Stop pushing and settle down!" "Josie, why haven't you brought your permission slip back in yet?"). Consider how this must wear on children—hearing their names used in negative ways more than in positive. And of course, it's the very children who most need a stronger positive identity who hear their names used negatively most often.

Alex, who I had one year in 5th grade, was just such a student. I'd say, "Hey, Alex. Come here for a minute," with the intention of having him share his poetry with me, and he'd explode, throwing his writing to the floor: "What the heck! I wasn't doing anything! Why is everyone always picking on me!" He was so used to being in trouble that it took months for me to be able to call him over for a writing conference without him exploding. Simply hearing his name spoken by the teacher was enough to put him into a panic.

It's also important to remember that we set the tone for all students in our class. Educator Andy Dousis wrote a powerful article, "What Teaching Matthew Taught Me," in which he reflected on how his frustrated and annoyed tone of voice modeled how to mistreat a student who so desperately needed positive social connections. He reflected, "it became clear that I was contributing to Matthew's mistreatment. But wait, let me be more precise: I wasn't just contributing to his mistreatment. I was teaching it. When I snapped at him, I gave permission to 23 others to snap at him too. I was using a surefire teaching strategy: modeling. . . . I realized that my interactions with Matthew were a powerful, unintentional modeling. When I stopped seeking Matthew out to say a friendly hello in the morning, the students stopped too. When I snapped commands at him, they snapped too. I was treated to a painful refresher lesson about the strength of modeling" (2007).

Let's make sure that all students hear their names used more in positive contexts than negative ones. Whenever possible, approach children who are struggling quietly and privately, instead of calling their names out across the classroom. By simply being nearby and making eye contact, you can communicate to the students without using their names, or at least doing so quietly. Make sure to go out of your way to use students' names positively as much as possible.

Naming a Group

We may also consider what we call groups of students, whether it's a whole class or a small group within the class. Many of the principles for naming individuals apply here too. Let's call students by respectful and empowering titles that improve their positive sense of self and emphasize attributes of the class that we want to encourage (see Figure 4.1 for examples). When considering what to call a class, you might ask yourself, "How do I want students to see (or think about) themselves?"

There are other creative ways of naming a group that you might consider. In the middle school that my children attended, the 5th grade team

FIGURE 4.1

Common Names for a Group	Potential Problem	Other Ideas to Consider
Boys and girls Ladies and gentlemen	This emphasizes gender as the defining attribute of students, which is probably not what we want to emphasize.	Scientists Readers Musicians Mathematicians Athletes Artists Everyone 4th graders Students Class
Mr. Robinson's class My class	This makes it sound like we own the students or like we are the defining characteristic of the class.	
Kiddos Little chicks Sweeties	This may feel condescending to students.	
Friends	Students aren't teachers' friends. Not all students are friends with each other. This can feel inauthentic.	

adopted a new totem animal each year and named itself after it. The name was unveiled in a grand naming ceremony a few weeks into the school year. In a charter school I once visited in Boston, each classroom in the 6th grade wing was named for a local college or university. When students changed classes throughout the day, they headed to Northeastern for math and Harvard for science and Boston University for literacy. The goal of this naming was to help students get used to the idea that college was within reach for all of them.

Another way to name a group, probably most appropriate in the elementary and middle school grades, is to have students create their own name. If you try this, make sure to take it slowly and help your students be thoughtful. Explain to them why they're going to create a team name—to build a sense of positive community, help name and celebrate positive goals and attributes of the class, and so on. Have them brainstorm and discuss names over several days. Feel free to veto any names suggested that you think are way off base, but do so respectfully ("I can see why Fluffy Pink Ninja Bunnies might be a fun name, but that doesn't fit our goals for naming our class"). Have the class come to consensus on a favorite name. Then, of course, work at using this name when referring to the group. "Okay, Team Challenge, it's time to head to lunch!"

Conclusion

I was working with a group of kindergarten teachers, and the issue of using terms of endearment with students came up. "I think it's the mother in me," one stated. "So many of our students don't get enough love at home. I call my students 'honey' and 'sweetie' just like I do my own children!" Her colleagues agreed, nodding vigorously. This is an extremely professional and thoughtful group of teachers who are ready to challenge and question their own practices, even if it's uncomfortable. And it *was* uncomfortable—as evidenced by what this teacher said next: "I'm willing to think about this, but my palms are sweating!"

You might be having similar struggles as you consider what you call your students. First and foremost, don't just change your practice right away—slow down and think for a bit. What are your goals for your students, and how does your language align with those goals? Are there tweaks and adjustments you might make to how you name students that might better align with your goals for them? If so, this might be a good goal to take on as a language challenge—to work at referring to students with names that will strengthen their positive identity so they are ready to take on the fun challenges that school presents.

5

Set Students Up for Success with Behavior

It was the first day of school in my first year as a teacher and we were about to head out of the classroom for the first time, so I said to my students, "You're in 4th grade, so you all know how to line up at the door respectfully and quietly. Let's go." I then watched in surprise as some students ran, shoving others out of the way. Others congregated in a clump near the door while a few lagged behind and didn't line up at all. *What's going on?* I wondered. *Didn't I just tell them to line up respectfully and quietly?*

Likely, there were several things going on. Students had a variety of teachers in 3rd grade who had different line-up procedures. Students likely also forgot some of how school behavior might be different from summer camp or home behavior over the course of the summer. After many such instances, I realized that I couldn't assume that my students knew how to behave in common school settings. More specifically, I learned that I couldn't assume that *all* my students knew how to behave in common school settings *the way I wanted them to*. I had to be clearer and more specific with my language.

There are other mistakes that we may make when trying to set students up for success with behaviors, routines, and social-emotional skills. We may accidentally focus on negative behaviors instead of positive ones, leaving students feeling dispirited or confused about what they should do. We may set unrealistic expectations, leading some students to feel defeated and to stop even trying to do the right thing. We might use wishy-washy language when we should be firm and clear, leading students to misunderstand directions. Overwhelmed by the frenetic pace of schools today, we might simply neglect to set students up for success at all, hoping they'll know what to do. The results of all of these mistakes are predictable: If we don't set students up for success, our classrooms feel chaotic and we spend way too much time putting out fires and reacting to behavior mistakes. So, let's explore a few key ideas about how our language can support students' positive behavior.

Hope Is Not a Classroom Management Strategy

Perhaps in an effort to keep a positive tone in the classroom, teachers sometimes shy away from talking too much about behaviors and expectations. Or, it might be that we're so pressed for time that we skip this crucial classroom management step, hoping or assuming that students will know how to manage themselves. This is especially common in middle and high school classrooms. However, if we don't set clear expectations for how a learning experience should look and feel, we leave much up to chance. Science materials turn into toys. Voices get too loud. Feelings get hurt. We can't simply hope that students know what to do. As I once heard a teacher say, "Hope is not a classroom management strategy."

To set students up for success, we need to think proactively: What should the experience look, sound, and feel like? We also need to anticipate what might be hard about following through on expectations: What might students struggle with? What might go wrong? We can then give directions and model behaviors, skills, and routines that students will need to behave appropriately. One group of middle school teachers I worked with called this "front-loading." In a discussion group, one of them, an 8th grade science teacher, recently said, "It's amazing how much better the kids do in an activity when I do a little bit of front-loading. They just know what to do."

Our first step as teachers, then, is to have a clear vision ours what an experience should be like. In Figure 5.1, notice how a teacher might think proactively by envisioning what an activity should look like and anticipating challenges.

FIGURE 5.1		
Learning Experience, Routine, or Activity	**What Should It Look, Sound, and Feel Like?**	**What Might Be Hard About This?**
Science lab	Active, interactive, purposeful, efficient, safe use of materials	Might get too loud, easy to get off track because students are talking with others
Writing rough drafts	Quiet, focused, centered on individual work with some conferences as needed	Hard to get settled or focused without too much talking
Transition from classroom to cafeteria for lunch	Quiet, calm, orderly, relaxed, efficient, respectful	Students can be cranky when hungry, have been sitting for a while, see friends or teachers in halls and want to talk
Band rehearsal	Purposeful, productive, friendly, supportive, playful	Can get loud and chaotic, some students have to wait while others play

Once we have figured out what we want an experience to be like and what might be problematic, we can then think about how to set students up for success through language. The following key ideas are the focus of the rest of this chapter:

- Focus on what to do (instead of what not to do).
- Set realistic and respectful expectations.
- Use a positive tone.
- Elicit ideas from students.
- Be direct and clear.

Focus on What to Do (Instead of What Not to Do)

One of the lessons I learned as a teenage lifeguard is that when stating expectations and reinforcing rules on the pool deck, it's better to focus your language on *what to do* instead of *what not to do*. For example, when reviewing rules with a group of kids at the start of a pool party, we were taught to state the positive expectation ("When you move about the pool deck, it's important to walk") instead of focusing on the possible mistake ("Don't run on the pool deck"). Similarly, once the party started and a kid was running, instead of calling out, "Don't run!" we were to call out, "Walk!" This is important for two reasons. The first is that to state what not to do is to leave open the possibility for other improper ways to travel around the pool. Kids might skip, leap, hop, or speed-walk. By stating a positive direction, you are clearer about the expected behavior. The second reason has to do with tone. It is more positive to focus on positive expectations rather than on rule-breaking or misbehavior. To the child who was running, "Walk!" is a reminder about what to do, while "Don't run!" is a public calling-out of improper behavior.

Additionally, when we state expectations in the positive, we show that we assume that students have the best of intentions, which helps set a respectful tone and climate of trust in the classroom. I remember how excited I was for science class my first day of 6th grade as a student. This was the first year we traded classes for different subjects, and it felt so grown up. The classroom *looked* like a science room: There were complex posters of anatomy on the walls, jars of animals in formaldehyde on shelves, and microscopes arranged in a line on top of a set of cabinets. Then our teacher began the first class with a lecture about how he kept his cabinets locked to make sure students didn't steal any of his science supplies, saying if he caught anyone stealing materials we'd be in big trouble. My heart sank. Here I was, bursting with excitement to learn about science, and my teacher already had his eye on me, expecting me to steal from him. I was crushed. Though I learned to enjoy science that year, I was never able to quite shake that feeling that I wasn't trusted. Notice that in Figure 5.2, the second statements emphasize positive behaviors and intentions.

FIGURE 5.2

Instead of . . .	Try This . . .
"When we're walking out to the field today, no one should be horsing around!"	"When we head out to the field today, make sure to stay with the group and keep your hands to yourselves."
"During a writing conference, you shouldn't just name all of the mistakes that someone makes, right?"	"During a writing conference, make sure to point out things your partner did well and a couple of ideas they could work on."
"It's getting too loud in here!"	"Keep voices between a whisper and a regular talking voice."
"Don't play with the science materials. These are tools, not toys."	"Remember to use the science materials appropriately. They need to stay on the table and only be used for our demonstration."
"During our class meeting, don't talk while others are talking. It's rude."	"During our class discussion, let's work at having one person share at a time. Raise your hand if you want to contribute an idea."

Are there times when we need to specifically name a negative behavior, though? What if there's something specific that we anticipate and want students to be aware of ahead of time? Certainly, this is sometimes the case. Part of effective classroom management is heading problems off at the pass—addressing them before they happen. So, let's explore some ways we can be both proactive and positive—how we can assume best intentions instead of worst—even as we anticipate student mistakes. Notice how the language in Figure 5.3 emphasizes empathy and kindness.

FIGURE 5.3

Instead of . . .	Try This . . .
"I'm going to be out of the room in a meeting this afternoon. I don't want to hear a report like I did last time. You shouldn't get wild just because I'm not here!"	"Remember how things got wild the last time I was out of the room in a meeting? Later today is a chance to try again. Let's figure some things out and start with why it can be harder to stay relaxed when someone new comes in."
"You better not light those Bunsen burners early!"	"It can be tempting to light the Bunsen burners as soon as you get to your lab stations. For safety's sake, wait until I give you the go-ahead."
"I better not see any fooling around during the concert this evening! You shouldn't be talking to your neighbor or waving to people in the crowd!"	"It can be really hard not to talk with your neighbor or wave to people in the crowd during a concert. Remember that even when you're not performing, the way you move is part of our whole performance."
"No running into the gym like a bunch of wild animals today!"	"When we've been getting to the gym, some kids have been running and sliding across the floor as soon as the door opens. Remember to walk to the circle area."

Set Realistic and Respectful Expectations

Just as it's important for us to have high academic expectations of our students, we should have high expectations for students' behavior. These expectations also need to reasonable—within realistic reach of our students. A common misstep that many of us have probably made is stating unrealistic expectations (ones that we know are too high) for students, hoping they'll then meet us in the middle, which was really our goal in the first place. For example, when some students are waiting for others to tune their instruments in band, we might say, "You should be silent while others are getting ready," figuring that if students whisper quietly, it will be good enough. You might wonder, as long as students are waiting respectfully, isn't that the point? Let's think about the message that we're sending when we say one thing but mean another. What students learn is that they can't meet expectations, and that it's okay to not really follow them. Instead, we should set clear limits and then follow through: "When you're waiting for others to tune their instruments, make sure to keep voices quiet so they can tune, and you'll be ready to play." Then, if students use voices that are too loud, we immediately give a little coaching to get them back on track. Now we're setting realistically high expectations and following through. Students can be successful, and they learn that we mean what we say and say what we mean. Figure 5.4 offers some examples of how this might sound.

FIGURE 5.4		
Instead of Unrealistically High Expectations	**Set Reasonably High Ones**	**And Follow Through as Needed**
"You should be silent when walking in the hallways."	"We should use quiet voices in the hallways."	"Remember that we need to use quiet voices in the hallways."
"No one should use phones or devices during this class period."	"Only use your phone or device to help with your learning this class period. Social media and music should be off."	"Brian, social media isn't an option today. Put your phone on my desk. You can get it back at the end of the period."
"Everyone should get at least three pages written in the next 45 minutes."	"Everyone should stay focused on writing for the next 45 minutes."	(To a table of three writers who are losing focus) "We have about 10 minutes to go. Try to get back on track!"

Use a Positive Tone

We should also be careful we don't slide into what I call the "tired TSA agent voice." Have you ever heard a security agent at an airport who's likely at the end of a shift (and has been saying the same thing over and over and over again for hours)? "Please remove all electronic devices bigger than a *cell phone*! Make sure to take off your *shoes*. Make sure to take off your *belts*!" The final word of each sentence is emphasized with exasperation. "You may not have any *liquids*! Take water out of your bags, and *drink it* or dump it in the *trash*!" It feels like they can't believe that after a four-hour shift, people still need to be reminded of the same thing (perhaps forgetting that people coming through the line are hearing this reminder for the first time that day).

I have found myself, as a teacher, sliding into this tone when tired and frustrated, but it's counterproductive and ridiculous. If we were to actually articulate what we're feeling, it might sound like our TSA agent friend: "I've been teaching for 10 years, and every year I have to model how to carry a chair safely. You'd think the kids would know this by now!" Of course, each year, our students will need the same procedures explained and modeled— it's all new to them. And, just like travelers who are thinking about many things all at once, friendly reminders about removing belts and watches is always helpful. A tone that is light and invitational—one that conveys the message "Hey, you probably already know this, but I thought you'd appreciate a nice reminder"—makes a big difference in travelers' moods and behavior. Aren't you more likely to be patient and empathetic with other travelers if you're treated with respect and dignity?

Elicit Ideas from Students

Another powerful way to set students up for success is to invite them to share their ideas about positive behavior. After all, although we shouldn't assume that all students know how to behave in any given situation, we also shouldn't assume that they don't know anything. In fact, students come to us with lots of experiences, positive skills, and good ideas about how to do lots of things in the classroom. We should tap into these ideas when teaching positive behaviors, boosting students' sense of competence and ownership of positive behavior by eliciting ideas from them.

Here are a few tips for asking for students' ideas in ways that support a positive community.

- Ask for ideas in the positive ("What should we do?" instead of "What shouldn't we do?"). If students state ideas in the negative ("We shouldn't call each other mean names"), help them turn the ideas around by asking, "What *should* we do?"
- Only ask for input if you're truly open to ideas and if you think students will be able to contribute appropriate ones. If you're looking for one specific idea, or if students won't have enough background experience to think of ideas, just name the positive expectation yourself.
- Focus on class rules and ideals instead of teacher demands when framing questions. This allows the behavior to be about responsibility to the rules as opposed to being obedient to the teacher. This can help avoid power struggles.
- Draw on students' past experiences to help trigger student ideas and promote a sense of growth and learning. Especially at the beginning of the year, this can help all students feel valued and that they have something to contribute to the class.

Here are some specific examples of these tips in action:

- **Computer lab.** "We'll learn so much more if we're efficient and productive today. What are some ideas you have for how we can do that?"
- **Book groups.** "Think back to yesterday's reading session. Some things went well, and some could have been better. What are some ways we can stay focused on reading and discussing books today?"
- **Class discussion to brainstorm ideas.** "How might our class rules help us have a respectful and productive brainstorming session—one where lots of different ideas get shared?"
- **Station activity in the art room.** "How can we be responsible during this station rotation?"
- **Introducing materials to students.** "I bet many of you have used protractors in previous years. What are some ideas you have for taking care of these so they'll last all year?"

Be Direct and Clear

One of the most important ways we can set students up for success when giving directions or instructions is to be direct and clear. As Ruth Charney emphasizes in *Teaching Children to Care*, we must say what we mean and mean what we say. This means avoiding some of the wishy-washy language habits that may sneak their way into our daily talk. Here are a few that are especially common.

Don't Ask Questions When Giving Directives

One of the most common mistakes we may make when managing the daily routines of the classroom is to use questions when we should be giving directions. We may do this to try and soften demands, making them feel friendlier and less assertive and harsh. "Would everyone please get out your research materials and get to work?" might feel gentler than, "Everyone get out your research materials and get to work." However, when we give directions by asking questions, we imply that students have the option to either follow the direction or not.

Another way teachers may ask questions instead of giving directives is by tacking on the word "okay" to directions. "We should all quiet down now, okaaaay?" Especially when used with an upturned sing-song voice, "okay" indicates that something is optional. In *Becoming a Successful Urban Teacher,* author and educator Dave Brown (2002) asserts that this kind of language is especially troubling when used by teachers from the suburbs in urban classrooms: "A concisely worded directive may sound rude to you, but for many urban children, this style of discourse is necessary for them to comply with your requests" (p. 73). He goes on to explain that when urban children don't follow through when given wishy-washy directives, their teachers may view them as uncooperative and insubordinate, while the students can't understand why they're in trouble.

Instead, we should use direct, clear, nonnegotiable statements with a firm and friendly voice so that all students can be successful (see Figure 5.5).

FIGURE 5.5		
Learning Experience	**Instead of . . .**	**Try This . . .**
Math activity	"Let's all try to be responsible with our dice, okaaay?"	"Make sure to use dice responsibly. Keep them on the table."
Preparing for a writing conference	"Can you all remember to write down your conference question before you meet with a partner?"	"Remember to write down your conference question before you meet with a partner."
History group discussion	"Can everyone try to contribute an idea to our discussion session?"	"Everyone should try to contribute an idea to our discussion."
After-school drama group	"No running around and being wild, all right?"	"Actors—be safe. Walk while on the stage."

Avoid Pseudo Open-Ended Questions

Here's a specific kind of question to watch out for. There are many times we might use open-ended questions to elicit ideas from students ("We're about to have a guest speaker join our class. What are some ways we can help her feel welcome and respected?"). However, when we want all students to hear and know the same direction—if there aren't many different possible answers to the question—we should be direct and clear and just tell them. If we ask a pseudo open-ended question (a question that sounds open-ended but really has just one correct response), we invite confusion and frustration.

Consider the example in Figure 5.6. In the first column, the students end up playing the "guess what the teacher is thinking game," which isn't much fun for students and wastes a lot of time. It also muddies the waters—potentially having students remember the wrong information.

FIGURE 5.6	
Instead of Using a Pseudo Open-Ended Question	**Consider Being Direct and Clear**
Teacher: If you're passing scissors to someone at your table, what's a good way to do that? Student: You could slide them across the table? Teacher: Nope. They might hit someone's hand. Someone else? Student: You could toss them really gently? Teacher: I hear you saying to be gentle, and that's on the right track, but tossing them still isn't safe. Who else has an idea? Student: You could pass them around the table? Teacher: I guess you could. I hadn't thought about that. But how should we pass them? Student: We should close them, hold them by the blades, and hand them to the person so they can grab the handles. Teacher: Yes!	Teacher: During today's activity, you may need to pass scissors to someone at your table. If so, close the scissors and hold them by the blades. Then, pass the scissors so they can be grabbed by the handles. Here, watch me as I demonstrate.

Avoid Please and Thank You

Let's be clear: We should model politeness. Students should learn how to use "please" and "thank you" in appropriate ways. However, it's almost always the case that when we need to set expectations, we *should not* use these terms. They can make statements feel weak or even ironic, softening requests or creating an unkind tone.

Much like asking a question in the wrong way, *please* can make a direction feel optional. "It's time to head back to your seats, please," makes it sound like a request that students can either follow or not. "Thank you for heading back to your seats" can feel a bit odd when it's stated as a request. Students might wonder, "Why is my teacher thanking me for something that hasn't happened yet?" I've even heard some teachers combine these terms: "It's time to head back to your seats, please and thank you!" Especially when used with a quick pert tone, this kind of language can put an emotional distance between students and teacher. There's something about it that feels dismissive.

When should we use these terms? When a request is truly optional, *please* is an appropriate polite term to use. "Would someone please stay in for recess today to help me clean the fish tank?" And if someone volunteers? Thank them! "Michaela, thank you so much for volunteering!"

Just Say "No"

There are times when we might see students start to do something they shouldn't or ask us permission for something that isn't okay. Again, in an effort to soften requests or redirections, we might be tempted to use negotiable language when we should be direct (see Figure 5.7). We might say "You probably shouldn't" when what we mean is "No." Remember, softening language often creates confusion or encourages limit-testing, which can erode the sense of safety you're trying to build with your students.

FIGURE 5.7

Situation	Instead of . . .	Try This . . .
Emma is working on a science project, and she asks if she can take an iPad home to keep working on the video she's producing.	"It's not really a good idea to take the iPad home. Something might happen to it."	"Nope. The iPads need to stay in school. How about we find a time when you could get some extra time to work. Maybe tomorrow afternoon?"
Addison is climbing up the slanted pole on the side of the swing set, laughing as the structure rocks back and forth. He looks like he's heading for the top.	"Hey, Addison! That's not really safe. Would you come on down, please?"	"Hey, Addison. Come down. You can climb on the jungle gym or the climbing wall but not on the swing set."
David asks, "Is it okay if we listen to some music while we work on our math problems?"	"I'm not sure you'll be able to focus with music on."	"Nope. During group work you need to be able to focus, and music will make that harder."

Conclusion

We know that when students are learning a new academic skill, whether it's long division, writing a persuasive essay, or a making a quick relay start in the pool or on the track, they are going to need lots of modeling, practice, and gentle guidance. We expect them to make mistakes and need coaching. We recognize that we won't be able to just tell them what to do and expect that to be enough. So, when it comes to helping students learn positive behaviors, we should keep these same things in mind—using language that is proactive and positive, clear and direct, firm and kind.

But what happens when we set students up for success with behavior and they still struggle? That is the topic of the next chapter!

6

Support Students When They Struggle with Behavior

In Chapter 5, we focused on how to set students up for success with various behaviors through our language. We explored how to be proactive and supportive so that students have a clear understanding of positive expectations. But what happens when they still make mistakes, even after all this careful and thoughtful proactive work? Let's be clear. No matter how well we set limits, teach positive behaviors, develop students' strong sense of self, and create a safe and collaborative community, students are still going to break rules and make mistakes. We should anticipate and even expect this. Long ago I heard Jim Fay, one of the founders of the Love & Logic approach to discipline, state this clearly: "If your kids are worth keeping, they're going to break the rules."

So how do we help students learn from mistakes and continue to support a positive classroom community? How do we continue to be clear and firm with expectations while also being respectful and kind?

Balance Firmness and Kindness

Have you seen the original *Mary Poppins*? Do you remember the scene when Mary Poppins arrives for her interview with Mr. Banks? It's hysterical.

While she reads aloud the job description point by point (a list of desired qualities that Jane and Michael wrote, which Mr. Banks tore up and threw in the fireplace), Mr. Banks grows increasingly agitated and confused, looking in the fireplace and bonking his head on the mantle. Mary Poppins, feigning confusion herself, wonders aloud if Mr. Banks is well. While all of this is going on there's a description of Mary Poppins' disposition that might serve as a model for speaking with children when they need help with discipline: "A cheery disposition—never cross but extremely firm."

Firm and kind is the perfect combination, but it's also a challenging balance. Kindness sets a tone of acceptance, positivity, and love. Firmness sets limits that help students feel safe. When teachers are kind but not firm, they appear weak and students feel insecure and uneasy. This leads to limit testing, which, if not stopped, leads to a greater sense of insecurity and more limit testing. Left unchecked, the classroom spirals out of control and learning all but stops. By contrast, if teachers are firm but not kind, students can fail to make important emotional connections with them. Because positive relationships with teachers are so important, students may disconnect from school, and again, learning shuts down. You've probably heard the adage: Students don't care what you know until they know that you care. So, let's channel our inner Mary Poppins and work at blending a cheery disposition with firmness. Spit-spot!

Address Small Issues Before They Escalate

Sometimes we wait too long to act, hoping students will get back on track on their own. For many students, this can backfire, leading them to get further out of control. We should use reminders and redirections to help students get back on track quickly.

Reminders help trigger what students already know and rely on students to regain self-control. They're especially useful when students are just about to (or are just in the process of) going off the rails:

- "Remember to use the lab materials safely."
- "Think back to what we said about how to be prepared for writing conferences. What do you remember?"
- "Hey, everyone. I notice that things are getting a bit wild as you're playing games. Who can remember some ways we can keep things calm?"

Redirections are, well, more direct. They tell students what to do and are best when they're short, clear, non-negotiable, and delivered in a firm and kind voice. These are especially helpful when students are off track and need a firmer tone to regain self-control:

- "Use the lab materials safely."
- "Go back to your seat and write your question for your conference before you sign up."
- "Freeze! Things are getting too wild. Bring your voices down and refocus on the games you're playing."

I was working with a new teacher recently, and we conducted a brief thought experiment. We imagined how a scene typically unfolds with a student who struggles with self-control when issues aren't addressed directly. It looked something like this:

Richard is wandering around the room when he should be working. The teacher ignores this, hoping that Richard will settle down on his own. Richard continues to wander and begins to distract other students, flicking their papers with his finger and humming loudly. The teacher asks Richard, "Would you sit back down please?" He complains, "I don't want to." He walks toward his seat but then veers away and keeps wandering and distracting. The teacher, trying to help other students (who are, of course, distracted by Richard's behavior), ignores Richard again, hoping he'll settle down. Richard, sensing that he doesn't have to follow through, feels a bit more edgy and gets louder as he walks from table to table. The teacher, getting frustrated, asks again, "Come on, Richard! You need to get to work, okay? Would you please settle down?" Richard, seeing that the teacher is hesitant to be firm, feels more unsettled. "But I don't want to!" he responds loudly. He now begins banging his hands on a nearby table and staring at the teacher. (It almost like he's screaming out, "Please make me stop!") Now the teacher, resentful that so much time and energy is being spent in this way, gets angry. "Richard! That's it! You don't have a choice! Get back to work or you're heading to the principal's office!" In this final abdication of authority, the teacher gets Richard, who sulks and pouts all the way, to sit back down, but only by reinforcing what they both already sense—that the teacher doesn't have any power or control.

We then backed up and imagined what might happen if the teacher had been more direct at the beginning of this scenario. It might have looked something like this:

Richard is wandering around the room when he should be working. The teacher moves over to Richard and says, "Richard, it's time to get back to work. Do you need help with anything?" A firm and clear voice communicates that this is not negotiable, and the teacher guides Richard back to his spot. Richard says that he is all set and gets back to work.

In the first instance, by ignoring and using weak language, the scenario escalates, taking much more time and energy and setting a tone of disrespect in the classroom. In the second case, by addressing things before Richard works himself up and becomes even more dysregulated, Richard gets back on track more quickly, and all students can stay focused on learning. Of course, the new teacher I was working with asked the question that you're surely thinking right now. What if, after the firm redirection, Richard refuses point-blank to do work and needs to be removed from the room? We talked about this and concluded that if it's going to happen one way or the other, it's better to be direct and have it happen more quickly so that the teacher can get back to teaching and all of the other students can get back to learning.

Address Issues Discreetly

As much as possible, we should redirect students in a one-on-one fashion. If students are starting to lose control, the last thing we want to do is create a public confrontation where an audience of students is waiting to see what happens next. For one thing, if other students are watching, they're not focusing on their learning. Additionally, if students now feel that peers are watching, they may attempt to save face by escalating the confrontation. Before we know it, we've got a very public power struggle on our hands. By pulling the student off to the side and setting limits without an audience, we're giving the student the opportunity to get control back and save face at the same time.

The exception to this rule is if a child has said something mean-spirited to another. For example, Harmony is walking in the hallway and Trisha sneers, "How many days this week are you going to wear the same sweater?" In this instance, we should address Trisha directly—and within earshot of Harmony and other students nearby who might have heard. If students think that a teacher has heard and ignored a mean comment, they may assume that the teacher is condoning that behavior. It's one of the things that can lead to an increase in bullying behaviors in schools (Englander & Schank, 2010). Even a short and clear type of response ("Trisha, unkind comments are not okay in this school!") will send an important message.

Anticipate Developmental Challenges

As a 4th grade teacher, I knew there were certain words that many 4th graders would typically misspell: *girl* (*gril*), *because* (*becuz, becuse, becaus*), and *could* (*culd, cud*) were just a few. These are common words that seem simple enough to an adult reader and writer, but for 9-year-olds, they can be tricky. It was important for me to keep in mind that every year, I should expect 4th graders to struggle with the spelling of these (and other) common words as they write. I should also expect them to be challenged by more abstract math concepts such as multiplication of fractions. I should expect them to be more interested in the drafting of writing pieces than in revising and editing. There are, of course, many positive characteristics to anticipate about 4th graders as well. As their reading becomes more fluent, they are able to build incredible reading stamina and dig into more interesting and complex literature. They have a passion for projects and game playing, which can add life and energy to the learning of almost any content.

I'll bet if you think for a moment, you can list some common academic challenges and strengths that are typical for the grades and ages you teach. Being in tune with developmental hallmarks of our students allows us to anticipate what we might need to teach. More importantly, it also enables us to treat certain academic challenges with understanding and empathy instead of frustration.

The same can then be true for behavior challenges. Just as we shouldn't react with scorn or frustration when a 4th grader spells *girl* as *gril*, when that same 4th grader gets highly agitated after ending up at the back of the lunch line, instead of being dismissive ("It doesn't matter. We're all going to the same place anyway!"), we can respond with empathy ("That can be frustrating. Let's have a class meeting later to figure out a fairer way to line up for lunch"). Do you teach 14-year-olds? Be ready to be patient as they struggle with organization and responsibility. Do you work with 6-year-olds? Be ready to be patient as they chew on sweatshirts and pencils—they're teething after all!

FIGURE 6.1		
Situation	**Instead of . . .**	**Try This. . .**
A 9-year-old is upset after ending up at the back of the line.	"It doesn't matter. We're all going to the same place anyway!"	"That can be frustrating. Let's have a class meeting later to figure out a fairer way to line up for lunch."
A 13-year-old forgets to bring back a permission slip on time.	"How many times do I have to remind you to bring in that slip? What's the matter with you?"	"What's a strategy you could use for remembering to get this slip signed—one that will work for you?"
A 7-year-old tells you that another child has sworn.	"Don't be such a tattletale! Mind your own business."	"You know that's not an appropriate word for school, don't you? You're showing you know the rule!"

Don't Overuse "Did You Make a Good Choice?"

Sometimes, in an effort to help students take responsibility for their actions after they've made a behavior mistake, teachers ask students, "Was that a good choice?" Though it's not the worst thing to say, it can be problematic. First off, when it's phrased as a yes or no question, there is really only one answer the teacher expects to hear, making it an inauthentic question. The children are supposed to hang their heads in shame and say, "No." What if the children think they made a good choice? Are we really open to a discussion if the child answers "Yes?" Second, there are many times when students don't actually make a choice with behavior. A classmate bumped into them, and they turned and shoved the classmate without thinking—it was simply a reaction. They didn't pause and consider the ramifications of shoving and decide that the pros outweighed the cons. The question, "Was it a good choice to shove Oscar?" implies intentionality when there was none. Instead, if we're trying to help the student think of ways to react differently in the future, we might say, "The next time someone bumps into you, what's a different way to respond—one that fits with our class rule about being safe and kind?"

Remember That Mistakes Are a Part of Learning

We would never try to set up a model of teaching academics where students aren't supposed to make mistakes. Mispronouncing words is a part of learning to read. Misplaying notes is a natural part of learning to play an instrument. Trying science experiments that don't come out the way we expect is a necessary part of the scientific process. If students work on math problems without making mistakes, they're almost certainly not growing as mathematicians. And (hopefully) we would never rely on criticism, sarcasm, or shaming as tools to help kids when they make academic mistakes. Imagine how harmful to learning it would be if we sat down for a writing conference with a student who is struggling with a first draft of a piece of writing and said, "What's the matter with you? Why can't you just get the draft written? How many times do I have to tell you to just write?!"

Unfortunately, students are routinely punished for making behavior mistakes. They are given punitive time-outs for calling out in class discussions instead of raising their hands. Students miss recess for not bringing in homework or for struggling to maintain attention in class. Kids get detentions for talking back or skipping class. The message here is clear: Mistakes are bad and to be avoided. Behavior incentive systems send the same message. In my first couple of years in the classroom, when I rewarded good-behaving groups with pizza for lunch, I reinforced the idea that mistakes were bad. If you made them, you were less likely to get a special lunch.

What do we say about behavior mistakes when we show annoyance, frustration, anger, sarcasm, disgust, or disappointment? Our emotions trigger predictable emotions for students: shame, embarrassment, resentment, fear, and anger. Is this our goal? It's pretty clear that if we want students to learn, these aren't the emotions we want them to have. In fact, these kinds of stress responses have been shown to have hugely negative effects on learning. As noted education and brain expert Eric Jensen states, "It can't be repeated enough: Threats activate defense mechanisms and behaviors that are great for survival but . . . lousy for learning" (Jensen, 1998, p. 57).

> ### A Bit of Advice About Consequences
>
> Consequences are an important part of discipline. They help set limits, which can be part of creating a safe environment. They can also (sometimes) be part of helping students learn positive behavior.
>
> Be careful not to over-rely on them, though.
>
> We know not to rely on circling spelling mistakes to help students learn to spell well. We need to teach phonemic skills, give students lots of coaching and support, and plenty of chances to read and write—a lot. Similarly, consequences are a small part of our approach to teaching positive behaviors, but they should not be the focus of our teaching of discipline.

This is true for all children, but it's especially true for children living with trauma and violence—students who are on the edge of fight, flight, or freeze all of the time. Unfortunately, these are the very children who likely struggle with emotional regulation in schools and will therefore tend to make more behavior mistakes than their peers. Traditional behavior management systems that rely on rewards and consequences can be especially challenging for students who struggle with emotional regulation. Ross Greene is specifically writing to parents in his powerful book, *The Explosive Child*, but his message holds true in the classroom as well: "Some . . . find that such programs actually *increase* the frequency and intensity of their child's explosions and cause their interactions with their child to *worsen*. Why? Because reward and punishment programs don't teach the skills of flexibility and frustration tolerance. And because getting punished or not receiving an anticipated reward makes kids feel more frustrated, not less" (Greene, 2005, p. 78).

So, through language that makes kids feel bad, we decrease their opportunities to learn and especially harm the children who most need help in the first place. How then should we react, and what should we say instead, when kids make behavior mistakes?

You might begin by considering how you want to be guided when you struggle with behavior mistakes. Let's consider a familiar scene at a staff meeting. A colleague, perhaps an administrator or another teacher, is sharing some important information with the faculty, but you're distracted. Your 13-year-old kid is home sick, and you're wondering how he's doing. You discretely slide your phone under the table and send him a text to check in. He responds, and you engage in a few minutes of back-and-forth communication. You lean in toward a colleague and ask her what you missed. Texting under the table and engaging in side conversations are both behaviors that you know are not appropriate for a staff meeting; they're ones that frustrate you when your students engage in them when you're teaching. So, if your principal were to address these behaviors with you, how would you want the situation handled? You'd probably want her to check in with you on the side discretely—not in front of your colleagues in the meeting. You'd probably also want your principal to assume that you had the best of intentions and not that you were intentionally being disrespectful.

I saw Kitri Doherty, a highly skilled teacher in Rollinsford, New Hampshire, use this strategy recently in a classroom, and it was a joy to observe. A 6th grade student was off-task. He was supposed to be writing for seven straight minutes to develop a "writing seed"—a piece of free writing that might be developed at a later point. Instead, he was on a laptop fiddling with the font of the title to a story he was already working on. He wasn't disruptive, but he was clearly not doing what he was supposed to be doing. Kitri approached this behavior problem in the same way she would an academic one—with a calm and relaxed demeanor (see Figure 6.2).

FIGURE 6.2

What She Could Have Done	What She Did
Loomed over student, folded arms, projected annoyance and frustration	Approached calmly, kneeled down next to student to be on eye level
Accused: "What are you doing? What are you *supposed* to be doing right now?!"	Asked: "How's it going?"
Likely Response	**Response**
The student probably would have shut down ("Nothing") or flared up ("I'm writing! Isn't that what we're supposed to be doing?").	He responded, "I didn't know what to write, so I did this." She responded, "Let me help you get going."

By approaching the student in a calm and invitational way, Kitri created an emotional climate where he could be responsive and relax. Instead of feeling threatened, as he surely would have if she had challenged him with an accusation, the student was open and able to explain what was getting in his way. Importantly, if Kitri had used anger and annoyance, he likely would have flared up and the situation would have escalated, not only further disrupting his learning but also distracting other students and raising their own anxiety levels—effectively reducing their ability to learn while increasing the probability of future confrontations with this student.

Let's consider some other common behavior mistakes and how we might respond to them (see Figure 6.3). Keep in mind that mistakes are a natural part of the learning process, and just like we do with academic mistakes, we should approach them with empathy and positive assumptions and see them as opportunities to coach and help students grow.

FIGURE 6.3		
Student Mistake	**Instead of . . .**	**Try This . . .**
Dropping a wrapper near the trash can but not in it	"Don't be so lazy! Pick up your trash!"	"Hey, Mike. You missed. Try again."
Flaring up at a partner during group work: "That's a stupid idea!"	"Hey, Jessie! Don't be so mean!"	"Jessie, take a break from the group for a minute. Then I'll help you think of a more respectful way to disagree with your partner."
Listening to music with an earbud instead of watching an instructional video	"Why am I not surprised! How many times do I have to tell you to put your phone away?"	"Pete, put your phone on my desk. You can get it on your way out of class."

Apologize When You Slip

It was mid-February. Haley wasn't working on her math, and I was frustrated and tired. She had called me over for help but then refused to listen, saying, "I don't care how you do it—just give me the answer!" I replied, "Nope. My job is to help you learn how to do it. Watch me as I solve this one." Haley ramped it up, "No! This is stupid. Just give me the answer!" I said, "I'll come back in a minute and we can try again." I took some deep breaths as I checked in with another student and then returned a minute later. She refused once again. "This is dumb. I don't want to know how to do it!" I reminded her of the system we had in place—a plan we had created together to help Haley when she was struggling: "Remember the deal, Haley. Work in the room or head to Lisa (the school counselor) and calm down, then come back and try later." She snarled and leaned in toward me sticking out her tongue—right in my face. I snapped. "Oh, that's nice!" I sneered. "What are you, 2 years old? Go to Lisa's office!" She threw her pencil and stormed out of the room.

I have to admit that for a brief moment, it felt really good to let her have it and lash out in anger. Then I felt horrible. What had been my intent? I was trying to hurt her feelings. Outraged at my own incompetence and feeling ineffective because I couldn't engage Haley, I lost my cool. Haley was the child in my classroom who least needed this kind of interaction. She had plenty of adults in her life modeling mean-spirited comments and emotional dysregulation, and it had always been my goal to show her that adults could be trusted to be kind and in control.

When Haley returned from the counselor's office about 20 minutes later, I was ready. I met her at the door with my right hand extended. "Haley, I am so sorry about what I said. I was frustrated. I've got to have more self-control than that."

We're all going to make mistakes. We will lose patience and say something we regret. Or, we'll lapse into permissiveness and allow things to get out of control. We might slip into sarcasm and hurt someone's feelings. It happens. And when it does, we must model taking responsibility for our mistakes and apologize in the most sincere and respectful way that we can. For this, too, can be an opportunity to model appropriate adult behavior.

Conclusion

I was recently observing in a school and started to notice lots of small misbehaviors percolating around the room. I wanted to capture some of what I saw, so I started taking some notes. Here's what I recorded over the course of about 30 minutes: side conversations, looking at phones under desks (texting and browsing social media sites), doing other work on the side, cracking jokes during conversations, coming in late, leaving early, passing a computer back and forth, coloring a picture (using multiple markers), talking over each other, sitting outside of the group, throwing a piece of candy across the room, interrupting others, and flipping a toy around and around. What's important to realize is that *this was a group of teachers*, not students! They were meeting to share strategies with each other about students who were struggling. What's also important to realize is that no one was being intentionally disruptive. No one was trying to ignore or interrupt someone else. These were just the little things that happen when a group of people get together.

We may find that we sometimes end up having higher expectations for our students than we would expect each other to be able to handle. Or, we may think that if we set students up for success, we shouldn't have to manage behavior mistakes once the year is well underway. Anytime a group of people get together to work and learn together, mistakes are going to happen. So, let's remember to keep our cool and smile as we redirect our students, helping them refocus and get back on track.

7

Elevate Students' Moral Reasoning

Some might argue that schools and teachers have no business involving themselves in the moral and ethical development of children. After all, isn't that the purview of parents and families? Shouldn't schools stick with educating students' minds and leave their moral development alone? Isn't this shaky ground?

Actually, we can't avoid it. The way we react (or don't react) to the daily situations of the classroom teaches a certain ethical or moral code whether we intend to do so or not. Let's say that a student makes a nasty comment to a classmate, and we respond, "Elyse, we only make kind comments in this classroom." We have just made an ethical statement: Unkindness is not okay. To ignore the comment and say nothing is also an ethical stance: Unkindness is acceptable.

Additionally, in order to create the safe and supportive environments needed for great learning to occur, we must ensure that student interactions are kind and cooperative. Teaching moral and ethical values are inherent in this process. In fact, most schools acknowledge this by creating schoolwide norms, rules, or codes of conduct. Though schools may adopt their own set of rules or guiding principles, they almost always include similar themes: respect for others, kindness, honesty, integrity, and other such universal moral values.

Understanding Stages of Moral Reasoning

Lawrence Kohlberg was a developmental psychologist at Harvard who has probably done the most important work in the understanding of moral development in children. He created a hierarchy of moral reasoning that can help us consider how we talk about moral and ethical behavior with students. The descriptions below are based on Kohlberg's work (1981), though they have been simplified a bit to be especially applicable in a school setting. They can help us consider people's moral reasoning—what's the right thing to do, and why? Once you become familiar with these levels, we can start to play with language patterns and where they sit on the hierarchy.

1. **Avoiding punishment.** In the lowest level of moral reasoning, people consider avoiding punishment as the primary goal. Students at this level, when deciding whether to walk or run in the hallways, will consider whether they'll get caught if they run. The driving question of this stage is, "Will I get in trouble?"

2. **Gaining a reward.** The next step up in moral reasoning is also based in self-interest: seeking rewards. Students at this stage might consider whether walking (instead of running) in the halls will gain them a good behavior ticket or earn points toward a class pizza party. The driving question of this stage is, "What's in it for me?"

3. **Earning praise/recognition.** In this next level, people are now motivated by social recognition and relationships. Earning praise or social status drives behavior. A student might reason, "If I walk in the hallways, I might get praised for being good." The driving question of this level is, "What will people think of me?"

4. **Following rules.** In this stage, people follow rules because that's what's needed in a civil society. If people don't follow rules, the reasoning goes, everything will fall apart. "If people run in the halls, the hallways will be chaotic." The driving question here is, "What if everybody did it?"

5. **Respecting all people.** In this stage, people focus on doing what's right based on the effect of their action on others or the greater good. Here a student might reason, "By walking in the hallways, I help others stay safe." The driving question here is, "How will my action impact others?"

Research has shown that facilitating classroom discussions about moral dilemmas can help children develop higher-level moral reasoning (Blatt & Kohlberg, 1975) and that children's moral reasoning can be elevated through discussion, which includes the presentation of higher-level moral reasoning (Walker & Taylor, 1991). It's pretty clear that the way we talk about moral reasoning has an effect on how students develop and grow in their moral development.

Too often in schools, even though we want students to think and act morally and ethically, we tend to emphasize low-level moral reasoning when we talk about behavior with them. "If you line up quickly, we'll put a marble in our marble jar," a teacher might encourage. "You'd better quiet down, or we're going to have to practice this during recess," a teacher may threaten. "If you can get your work done quickly, you can have some free time at the end of class," a teacher might bribe. Perhaps we're working hard to manage students instead of teaching them when it comes to behavior. After all, this kind of language often brings more immediate results—a threat or a bribe gets students attention in the short term. Perhaps we're stuck in the habit of addressing the whole class with the few in mind who most struggle—the ones who seem to need lower-level reasons (avoiding punishment or gaining rewards) for positive behavior. Whatever the reason, when we articulate low-level moral reasoning for why students should (or shouldn't) do something, we're reinforcing low-level moral reasoning. We send the message that the reason to do the right thing is to get a treat or avoid a consequence. If we want students to learn to do the right thing even when no one's watching, clearly these language habits don't fit.

Let's consider how encouragement might sound and feel at different levels of moral reasoning. We'll use an example that many of us are familiar with: You have to be out of the classroom for a while, and you want to encourage respectful and responsible behavior while the guest teacher is in the room. (On a side note, notice that "guest teacher" had a very different feel from "substitute teacher" or "sub.") I suggest reading Figure 7.1 beginning at the bottom and working your way up.

FIGURE 7.1	
Moral Rationale	**Why Should We Be Kind and Respectful of a Guest Teacher?**
Respect others	"Being kind and respectful is a way we can help our guest feel valued. It helps our classroom be a welcoming place for all!"
Follow rules	"Our rules say to be kind and respectful. We should follow that with our guest teacher this afternoon."
Earn praise/recognition	"I would be so proud of you if you would be kind and respectful to our guest teacher."
Gain reward	"If you're kind and respectful, we'll add another couple of stickers to our sticker chart. We're almost up to our next ice cream party!"
Avoid punishment	"If you are rude and disrespectful, you'll lose recess the next day."

Notice how different this feels and sounds as we move up the ladder? Although in every instance we're encouraging kind and respectful behavior, we're emphasizing a different reason for doing so. In a moment, we'll explore a couple of common language habits that tend to sit fairly low on Kohlberg's hierarchy and consider how we can help elevate students' moral reasoning through different language. First, however, we need to briefly discuss the role of rules in school, for the kinds of rules we have can dramatically affect the language we use.

When I was growing up, classroom rules were created by the teacher and told me what not to do. "Don't talk out of turn. Don't run in the halls." Following these rules was an exercise in compliance to adult authority and mainly focused on a system of rewards and punishments. If you broke a rule, you got your name on the board as a warning. A check next to your name meant you stayed after school for a detention. In this case, using the language of following the rules is still going to feel fairly low on the moral hierarchy. "Our rules say to walk single file with no talking!" is about compliance for the sake of obedience. A simple shift in where rules come from can make a profound difference.

When rules come from students' and teachers' visions of how we want our classrooms and schools to be, following the rules is much more than an exercise in compliance. Indeed, when following the rules is about working toward our goals of treating others with respect, creating a safe and joyful learning environment, and striving to do great work, following the rules now approaches the top of the moral reasoning hierarchy. When we say, "Remember that one of our rules is to show respect for others. How can we do that as classmates share a piece of writing with the class?" we're encouraging students to live up to their highest ideals articulated in their rules. Keep this in mind as you explore the next few sections of this chapter. Whenever mention is made of rules, know that the reference is to rules created by and with students—rules that focus on helping students envision and live up to their highest ideals for the ways school should be.

Let's now examine a few key suggestions and goals we might have for our language if we want to help elevate students' moral development.

Rethink the Language of Incentives and Consequences

- "If you work really hard during this next math period, then we'll have time for a game at the end!"
- "If you walk quietly in the hall on the way back from music, then we'll put another gem in our gem jar!"
- "If you can't settle down and get to work, you're going to have to finish that work during your recess."
- "If you don't put your phone away right now, then I'm going to take it away."
- "If you want to get a good grade, you'd better study for the test."

Perhaps one of the most prevalent language habits in schools is the if-then language of the threat of consequences or the promise of rewards. I see this in rural, urban, and suburban schools at the preschool, elementary, middle, and high school levels. Although we all want students to grow in their capacity to do the right things for the right reasons, these if-then statements feed them a steady diet of low-level moral reasoning for everything they do.

This language is problematic for other reasons as well. First of all, it takes behavior that could be personal or relational—about how we take care of ourselves or others—and makes it transactional. Instead of potentially thinking about how students' actions might affect others or their own long-term goals, they end up thinking about what they might get or lose in the moment. Instead of thinking about respecting others while walking in the halls, they're thinking about stickers on a chart. Instead of thinking about learning for growth, they're thinking about not losing their phone or getting a grade. So, what happens when that sticker or grade doesn't matter? A kid might (rightly) reason, *if I don't care about getting a sticker, why should I walk quietly in the hall?*

In a fascinating study in Israel, parents who were fined for picking their preschoolers up late from school showed up late more often (Levitt & Dubner, 2005, pp. 19–20). Instead of thinking about being respectful of teachers, they were left considering if a monetary fine was a compelling enough reason to be on time. In fact, parents decided that they'd happily pay some extra money for a bit more time before pick-up in the afternoon. A classic result of incentive- and punishment-based programs in schools is that once students have experienced the rewards and punishments, they often become habituated to them, and rewards and consequences have to be amped up to make an effect on short-term behavior. This is why schools that use incentive systems often find themselves constantly upping the ante to try to find the next reward that will motivate students.

Importantly, these kinds of systems also decrease intrinsic motivation. Study after study has shown that when you reward someone for doing something, you devalue what you meant to incentivize. So, if your goal is to boost children's enjoyment of reading, offering them pizza gift certificates for reading over the summer may actually decrease their desire to read. If you want to get kids to bring in their homework for the sake of responsibility and learning, offering them extra recess for bringing in their homework may decrease their motivation to bring in their homework. (For a thorough examination of this topic, consider exploring *Punished by Rewards* by Alfie Kohn.) We'll explore this in a bit more depth in Chapter 11 when we look at boosting intrinsic motivation.

If we're not going to use the if-then language of rewards and punishments, incentives and consequences, what should we use? We can try moving up the moral hierarchy and considering language that focuses on following rules and taking care of others. We might also use language that emphasizes the values we want students to share: learning for the joy of learning. Figure 7.2 includes a few ideas for how that might sound.

FIGURE 7.2	
Instead of . . .	**Try This . . .**
"If you work really hard during this next math period, then we'll have time for a game at the end!"	"Working really hard during this next math period is the key to understanding this new concept!"
"If you walk quietly in the hall on the way back from music, then we'll put another sticker on our sticker chart!"	"Let's remember to walk quietly in the halls. That will help other classes focus on learning as we pass by."
"If you can't settle down and get to work, you're going to have to finish that work during your recess."	"Try and settle down so you can refocus on your work. Remember that we just have one more week to work on this project!"
"If you don't put your phone away right now, then I'm going to take it away."	"This is a time when phones need to be put away."
"If you want to get a good grade, you'd better study for the test."	"Studying for this test is a way you can consolidate learning to help the learning go deeper."

This, of course, doesn't mean that we no longer use consequences as a part of daily discipline. Quite the contrary. Consequences can be an effective way to stop behavior mistakes before they escalate or help students regain self-control. They set limits to help a learning environment stay safe and productive. So, if the student doesn't put her phone away, we might say, "Quinn, hand me your phone. You can have it back at the end of class." Similarly, we might occasionally celebrate hard work and positive behavior with a fun treat. "Wow! We have put in such incredible work this afternoon! Let's head outside for a quick game!" The key shift here is in how we talk about the connection between behavior and consequences or celebrations. When we use if-then statements, we're implying that the reward or consequence is the reason for the behavior. We're trying to motivate students by using carrots and sticks, and this is where the damage is done.

Another common question about if-then statements is whether they ever be used, especially ahead of time. Don't we want kids to know about (and consider) consequences—both good and bad—of their actions? Isn't it unfair to have kids suddenly experiencing consequences without knowing about them ahead of time? Again, we have to think about our goals. When we try and motivate behavior with the language of carrots and sticks, we may give students the impression that the carrot or stick is the reason for doing the behavior ("Clean up your work space to earn tickets toward the prize box"). I think discussing possible consequences of behaviors with students is important. Especially at the beginning of the year, when creating rules with a class, a discussion about the role consequences will play in the daily discipline of the room can be supportive and reassuring for kids. It's one of the ways we let them know that we're going to keep the room safe. "We're all going to work at using devices in ways that support our learning this year. If someone is having a hard time with that—let's say someone is on social media when they should be writing—then they might lose their device for a while, so they can refocus on work." Notice the if-then statement in that last bit of language? When used ahead of time, to give students a heads-up, and when used with a supportive tone, these kinds of statements can help students understand and anticipate how the room will work. Once we're in the heat of the moment, however, it's best to avoid these statements—just act.

Rethink Praise and Disappointment

Another pattern of language that is just as prevalent as the language of punishments and rewards is the language of praise and disappointment. While if-then language controls students through punishments and rewards, the language of praise and disappointment controls them through the relationship between child and teacher.

- "I like the way you are putting such great effort into this piece of writing!"
- "Sam, I love how you just held the door open for Julian. Great job!"
- "Liza, I appreciate how well you're working with your group right now!"
- "I was watching how you all behaved during the schoolwide assembly we just had, and I am very disappointed."
- "I shouldn't have to explain directions five times. Why can't you all just listen the first time?"

When we think about these kinds of statements in terms of the moral hierarchy, we can see that they're one step above the levels of reward and punishment, but we can still do better. These kinds of statements use the personal relationship with the teacher as the driving motivation for engaging in appropriate behavior. Why should we work well with others? Why should we listen to directions? Because it makes the teacher happy when we do so. Instead of thinking about the greater good—working well with others helps us all learn more and listening to directions gets us ready for great learning—kids are now thinking about how the teacher feels. While this may seem to work in the moment (especially with younger children), there's once again no motivation for doing the right thing when no one's watching. Another danger is that students may think that our love and caring for them is conditional. If they're "being good" we like them, but if they're "being bad" we don't. If we want students to begin to think at higher moral levels, we should use language that will help them get there. See Figure 7.3 for some ideas of how to rework the language of praise and disappointment to move up the moral reasoning hierarchy.

FIGURE 7.3	
Instead of . . .	**Try This . . .**
"I like the way you are putting such great effort into this piece of writing!"	"You're putting such great effort into this piece of writing. That's going help you create a great final story!"
"Sam, I love how you just held the door open for Julian. Thank you!"	"Sam, that was really helpful when you held the door open for Julian. I bet he appreciated that!"
"Liza, I appreciate how well you worked with your group today!"	"Liza, you worked so well with your group today. That helped you all get a lot done!"
"I was watching how you all behaved during the schoolwide assembly we just had, and I am very disappointed."	"We didn't live up to our class rules at the assembly today. Let's talk about what we can do better next time."
"I shouldn't have to explain directions five times. Why can't you all just listen the first time?"	"It's time to refocus—people are having a hard time listening to directions and that's going to make it hard for you to know what to do in this next activity."

Does this mean that we should never betray our emotions—that our students shouldn't know if we're happy or proud or upset or disappointed? Of course not. It's just that we shouldn't intentionally use our relationships with students to manipulate their behavior. We don't want students, when thinking about what to do, to consider it through the lens of, "What will Mr. Anderson think?" This means that they're not really thinking for themselves. Also, if this is the reasoning, there's a next logical step: "He'll never find out!" If there's no deeper moral compass to guide behavior, students can easily make poor decisions.

Use the Language of the Rules

Again, we should explore the power of developing rules with students. When the anchor of discipline in the classroom is the teacher, we may unintentionally invite power struggles. "I need you to use a respectful tone" indicates that the student should be respectful because the teacher

Steps for Creating Rules *with* Students

1. Have students articulate their vision for an ideal classroom. What would it look, sound, and feel like?

2. Brainstorm ideas for rules that will support that ideal vision.

3. Gain consensus on a few rules that students agree they should work toward.

4. Post these in the room, and refer to them throughout the day as a guide for all members of the class.

is demanding it. When we use the language of the rules as the anchor of discipline, we create a less confrontational situation when a student needs support and direction. "Our rules say we should respect others" still allows the teacher to redirect a student who is struggling, but the emphasis shifts from following teacher demands to following the rules of the room. When teachers take time to create rules with students, and the rules flow from students' positive goals and visions for creating a safe and inclusive classroom, this is especially powerful. We can also use the language of the rules proactively, helping students use the rules as a guide for positive behavior. Consider how in each of the examples in Figure 7.4, expectations are still high, and the teacher is still supporting positive behaviors while doing so in a less confrontational way.

FIGURE 7.4	
Instead of . . .	**Try This . . .**
"I need you to clean up your lab supplies by the end of the period."	"Remember our class rule about taking care of the room. Make sure to clean up your lab supplies."
"Remember my rule about cleaning up your work area. I expect tables to be clean before you leave for lunch."	"Remember our class rule about taking care of our classroom. Make sure to clean your tables before you head to lunch."
"Hey! Why are you running in the halls? I need you to stop and walk!"	"Stop! We've got a school rule about being safe in the halls. Walk."
"I don't care for that language or tone of voice, young man!"	"Mike, remember to use respectful language, even when you're upset."

What About the Golden Rule?

Many classrooms adopt the Golden Rule as a guiding principle of the class-room. Shared by nearly every major religion in some form or other, the Golden Rule is familiar to most and is often accepted as a classroom rule quickly and easily. It's usually stated as some version of "Treat others the way you want to be treated." It was nearly always suggested by my students as I generated rules with them at the beginning of the year.

The Golden Rule can offer students an opportunity to practice empa-thy—to understand how their actions might be felt by others. In a class dis-cussion about teasing, a teacher might pose the question, "How would it feel for you if everyone made fun of you after you got a new haircut?" When used in this way, the Golden Rule might help elevate students' moral thinking, moving them from only thinking about themselves to being able to think about others.

There's a caution here, though. When discussing whether swearing is okay on the playground, a student might rationalize, "I don't mind swearing, so it's okay for me to swear." Here we see a potential drawback of the Golden Rule. Instead of helping this student practice empathy, it helps justify his self-centered viewpoint. In light of this, when I had a class that insisted on adopting the Golden Rule as a class rule, I offered a tweak that they always accepted. Instead of "Treat others the way *you* want to be treated" we would adopt "Treat others the way *they* want to be treated." This allowed the rule to serve as a moral guide for behavior while also focusing the rationale on what was desired by others.

Conclusion

We all want students to engage in positive behavior for the right reasons. At its most basic level, positive behavior is required for effective class-room management. We need students to be respectful and responsible so the day runs smoothly and we can work on the great learning at hand. It's also important to remember that the social and emotional skills of self-regulation, cooperation, collaboration, empathy, responsible decision making, and many more are core skills that students need to be successful in school today and in work tomorrow. Finally, good behavior should be so much more than not getting in trouble, getting prizes, and showing blind compliance to authority. We want our students to grow in their capacity to think and reason morally so they can act in thoughtful and ethical ways.

There are a few key language habits we might consider as we help create schools where this can happen. By emphasizing higher-level moral reasoning as we articulate why certain behaviors are (or aren't) expected, we can help students move beyond carrot-and-stick compliance. When we think of behaviors as skill-based, just as we do academics, we can approach the teaching of positive behavior in more holistic and empathetic ways. And finally, we can remember that the way we conduct ourselves sets clear models for how kids should conduct themselves as well. We should remember that they are always watching us—trying to figure out what it means to be an adult.

8

Promote Joyful Learning

You walk into Kathy Bresciano's and Suzanne Ryan's classrooms and are immediately struck by the energy and enthusiasm with which students work. Students sustain focus and attention for prolonged periods of time. They are independent and work with purpose. They solve problems creatively, engage in energetic conversations about their learning, and are truly self-directed. They see themselves as learners, are intrinsically motivated, feel ownership of their work, and are joyful about learning. As you read this description, you might sigh and think, "Oh, wouldn't that be nice! I'd settle for a tenth of that positive energy!" For Kathy, Suzanne, and many other preschool teachers out there, this day is like practically every other. Each day their students show up to school ready to engage in joyful work.

So, what happens to children's zeal for learning as they progress through school? Why do so many children seem to lose their love of learning as they move from preschool through elementary school and into middle and high school? Of course, there are many factors that we don't have time to get into in this book—developmentally inappropriate practices pushed by standardized testing and rigid scripted curricula and pacing guides is one. But what if the language we use with students—the way we talk about learning on a daily basis—also plays a part? Without meaning to, we may talk about school and work in ways that diminish students' enthusiasm for learning.

For example, when I was a young teacher, I would say things like, "Okay, everyone. If we work really hard and get through this math work, we'll do something fun afterwards." I meant to boost energy and enthusiasm, and I suppose that sometimes happened in the short term, but at what long-term cost? Consider the underlying message. When I talked about "getting through math" so we could "do something fun" I was sending the message that math wasn't fun. It was a chore—something that we did because we had to—something that stood between us and fun.

It took me a while to recognize that these kinds of messages communicate that work is distasteful. I shouldn't have been surprised when some kids groaned as math rolled around. Eventually, I realized that if I wanted my students to love learning, I needed to start paying attention to the messages I was sending. This had a profound influence on the way I talked about learning with my students. Now, as an education consultant, when I work in schools and observe in classrooms, I'm always on the lookout for examples of language that send positive messages to students about learning. I'm excited to share many ideas for you to consider.

Use Positive Messaging

According to Dan Pink, we're all in sales now. In his best-selling book, *To Sell Is Human*, he talks about the challenge that teachers face. We must convince students "to part with resources—time, attention, effort" (2012, p. 39). This can be challenging, to say the least, and some students appear to be reluctant to part with these resources. What we must do, then, is to convince students that their time, attention, and effort are worth spending. The way we talk about academic work is an important part of this effort. I was teaching a demonstration lesson involving choice in a high school algebra class recently. I had put together a resource for students to use to practice solving problems using order of operations. The resource had a variety of problems of different complexities and challenge levels, and I was teaching students how to make good choices about finding problems to solve that were in their just-right challenge zone. "Find problems that give you a fun challenge," I invited, "ones that give you enough of a push to make you sweat a bit but that are also within your reach."

All of the math teachers at this school observed the lesson, and afterwards, the head of the math department gently pushed back on the language I had used: "You used that term 'fun challenge' to describe the problems they should choose. But what if some kids don't find challenges fun in math?" I responded, "I *want* students to recognize that challenges can be fun in math, so I used the term 'fun challenge.'" By framing challenges as fun, I hope that a bit of this rubs off on students.

The key to using this kind of teacher talk effectively is that it should be subtle. There's a fine line here between being positive and engaging in thought control. We don't want to belabor or overdo this kind of talk because it will sound forced or inauthentic. It's also important to recognize that the statement must be true. If we say that a boring worksheet will be super fun, we may lose a bit of respect and trust from our students. Don't put lipstick on a pig. Let's work at actually making sure the learning activities we're facilitating are enjoyable.

Exude Joy, Passion, and Wonder

Wendy Stough, a 1st grade teacher in Nashua, New Hampshire, is working with a small group of readers at a table in the back of the classroom. Students are on a scavenger hunt in their reading books looking for compound words and contractions. Students are getting more and more excited as they find these words in their books, and Wendy's expression and interest match her students'. Her eyes sparkle, and her tone radiates enthusiasm. At one point, a boy turns to her in wonder and exclaims, "There are so many!" Wendy nods and smiles, replying, "The contractions and compound words are everywhere. They're thick!" In this simple small moment, we see a teacher who is excited about learning and teaching. Her spirit is infectious and helps set a tone of joyful learning with her students.

The best teachers are great learners. What better way could there possibly be to promote joyful learning in your classroom than to model it whenever possible? Teacher talk is one way to do this, and like all other kinds of language, tone of voice and body language are important. An upbeat and lively voice transmits joy. Leaning in toward students and their work shows interest.

I saw another example of this in a science class at Massabesic High School in Waterboro, Maine. Heather Sawyer's high school forensics class (why didn't my high school offer forensics?) was investigating properties of different fabrics by examining samples under a microscope and performing a simple burn test with a Bunsen burner. Heather moved around the room, supporting and encouraging lab partners in their work:

- "Isn't that cool?" she crooned as a student showed her something in a microscope.
- "I don't know. I'm stumped!" she replied in answer to a question from a student about why water seemed to change how the fabric looked under the microscope.
- "Oh, so you think you have it?" she asked as a student shared a hypothesis.

Her tone was open, upbeat, inviting, and quizzical. With every interaction, she helped set a tone of intellectual curiosity.

In his book *Engaging Students with Poverty in Mind* (2013), Eric Jensen highlights the importance of teachers setting the right tone for students. He acknowledges that many students come to school with less than ideal emotional states: Apathy, resentment, boredom, hopelessness, and mischievousness are just a few. He lists what he calls *target states*, the states that will help kids learn, and this list will serve us here as the tones we can model to promote joyful learning: anticipation, confidence, curiosity, suspense, inquisitiveness, intrigue, expectancy, puzzlement, and challenge (p. 41).

Here's a quick exercise to try. First, jot down some positive emotional states that you want your students to experience as they learn. (You might begin with some from Eric Jensen's list!) Put each of these ideas on its own line on a piece of paper or in a table in a document. Now, jot down an idea or two of things you could say that feel natural for you and would show your emotional state. Consider Figure 8.1.

FIGURE 8.1	
Desired Emotional States	**What You Might Say to Demonstrate Each State**
Intrigue	• "No kidding! How did you figure that out?" • "Are you serious!" • "Oh my gosh!"
Anticipation	• "I'm so excited to see where we go next with this project. I can't wait to get back to it tomorrow!" • "What do you think we could accomplish by the end of next week?" • "Oh, I just can't wait to read this next chapter!"
Passion	• "I just love science—it's so cool to learn how the world works!" • "How amazing is this?" • "Don't you just love the feeling you get when you come up with a new idea as a writer?"

Share Your Own Stories of Engaged Learning

Think about times you have been joyfully engaged in learning. Examples from your own school experiences might come to mind. Or, you might think of examples from outside of school (e.g., from a sport, craft, or hobby). Find ways of bringing these stories into the classroom so that your students get to see you talking with joy and positive energy about learning.

The story doesn't even have to be about the particular skill or content you are teaching. For example, you might be teaching students about the importance of practice as a musician and then reinforce this with a story about your own experience as an athlete: "As a runner, I know that daily practice is what builds skill over time. I had a goal of running a half marathon, so I carved out time every day to exercise. It was hard at first, but once I got into the habit, it became something I looked forward to. Some days it's still hard to force myself to lace up the sneakers, but once I get outside and get going, I enjoy it!"

Talk Positively About School

How do we talk about school in general? Do we use language that conveys our own positive feelings about school, or do we accidentally send messages that say the reverse?

What message do we send, for example, when we pray for a snow day? There's nothing wrong with enjoying the break in routine and the gift of a snowy day with a good book in the middle of the week. I think there's no real harm in sharing our excitement with our students. Consider, however, the difference in the following messages in Figure 8.2:

FIGURE 8.2	
Instead of . . .	**Try This . . .**
"Okay, everyone. Let's all pray for a snow day. Make sure to put spoons under your pillows and wear your PJs inside-out to bed so we can have a day off tomorrow!"	"A snow day would be fun, but I'd hate to miss a day with you all tomorrow. We're doing such cool work on our research projects, and I'd hate to lose any momentum!"
"I know we all can't wait for vacation in a few days, but let's see if we can power through and stay focused."	"I can't believe we only have a few days until vacation! We have so much great work still to do!"

While the messages in both columns are upbeat and positive, those in the second one send the loud-and-clear message that the teacher wants to be in school. So, take down your sign that reads "Pray for snow. I'm a teacher" and hang it in your bedroom at home! You can keep it near your coffee mug that says "The best two things about being a teacher are July and August."

Be Playful

Jen Blair's calculus students were graphing equations, and they were struggling. Tension was building as students were on the edge of understanding but not quite there yet. Jen posed a question to the class to help them remember some problem-solving strategies they had been working on: "So, how can you handle this problem if you have no idea how to do this?" A student responded, "Cry a little?" Jen, without missing a beat, and with a twinkle in her eye, responded, "Sure. As long as it's only a little bit. What would you do next?" A collective chuckle rippled through the class. With one brief moment of levity, Jen reduced anxiety and helped everyone relax—resetting the climate of the room so students could reengage in learning.

Earl Hunter II teaches 5th grade in Los Angeles. He has a robust voice that exudes warmth and a passion for learning, and he sprinkles small moments of playfulness throughout his teaching. I watched as he facilitated a math discussion and noticed how these small comments added an undertone of joy to the classroom. When the class is struggling with a concept, Earl strikes the tone of an ancient mystic: "Ah! Confusion abounds!" When he's looking for students to share ideas, he asks, "What say you?" Students roll with these comments (sometimes rolling their eyes), chuckling or just letting them slide by. They add little sparks of interest to the class.

For many students, humor is a gold standard. I can't count the number of times my son has come home from school with some version of, "Mrs. Jenkins is awesome. She's so funny!" This doesn't mean that we all need to be stand-up comics. In fact, too many jokes and laughs distract from learning—getting students overly silly or off-task. The key is to use humor sparingly—just enough to keep the energy playful but not enough to overwhelm.

You may be wondering, but what if I'm just not funny at all? First, this section is titled "playfulness" and not "humor" for a reason. While not all of us may consider humor a strength, we all have the capacity to be playful. Second, if playfulness isn't currently a strength, like any other skill it can be learned, practiced, and developed.

To get you started, here are a few more examples of playful language that I've seen in other classrooms:

- A kindergarten teacher wanted to encourage her students to pay attention to something she was explaining. She brought her hands up to her eyes like binoculars and said, "Okay, everyone. Put on your attentoscopes!" Students giggled as they looked through their hands at her.

- A 4th grade teacher was modeling a math problem on the board. Sensing that a few students were drifting, he got a bit playful with his example. "Shane (a student in the class) has oatmeal every morning for breakfast." Shane laughed and protested: "No, I don't!" Kids perked up, chuckling, and the teacher continued with a wink. "He doesn't just eat it plain, though. He loves to add things. If he has 35 crickets mixed into his oatmeal every day for 5 days, how many crickets will he eat?" "Ew, gross! Shane!" a few students laughed. Shane started playing along. "Mmmm. They're crunchy!" The teacher tapped into the students' energy. "Okay everyone, pick up your dry-erase boards and see if you can solve this challenge."

- An 8th grade teacher was giving a brief lecture about the American Revolution before students reengaged with their simulation. Perched on his favorite swivel stool in the front of the room, he pivoted 90 degrees so that students could see him from the side. "Here's a side story," he began before launching into a quick tangent.

- A chemistry teacher sprinkled wry puns and jokes into daily lessons. "Max Planck was *board* with his name." "Don't trust atoms. They make everything up." "Why do chemists enjoy working with ammonia? Because it's pretty basic stuff." Soon, students were looking up jokes and bringing them into class to share.

Conclusion

A colleague once accused me of being an old fuddy-duddy who didn't want kids to have fun in school. Halloween was approaching, and I was grumping about the time lost to academics. Our school had a tradition of having kids dress up and walk the neighborhood, so not only did we lose a whole afternoon of learning, but it was also hard to get much done earlier in the day because kids were so juiced up in anticipation of the parade. I struggle with spending school time on Halloween, Valentine's Day, and other such holi-days. It's not that I have anything against those holidays in general, it's just that as a teacher, I find them a distraction and a waste of time. They always seem to take time and energy away from projects and more important work. Even when I find ways of connecting these days to learning activities—read-ing and writing suspenseful stories around Halloween, for example—it often feels forced. My colleague rolled her eyes and groaned, "But, Mike, come on! School shouldn't just be about work all of the time. Kids need to have some fun too!" It was that comment that helped me understand our disconnect. I don't view schoolwork as drudgery. I don't feel the need to take a break from work to let my students have fun because I think *the work itself should be fun*. The more we can practice language habits that support joyful learning in our classrooms, the more our students will also view learning and school as inherently pleasurable and worthy of their emotional energy and intellectual attention.

9

Increase Student Ownership of Learning

Take a look at Figure 9.1 and see if you can find the differences between language examples in each column.

FIGURE 9.1	
Instead of . . .	**Try This . . .**
"I have an exciting math activity planned for you today!"	"You're going to get to try an exciting math activity today!"
"I'm going to show you the three criteria for quality work that I expect you to meet in this next project."	"Let's think together about what we want to see in work if projects are going to be high-quality."
"Thank you so much for putting in so much effort on that last writing assignment!"	"Wow! You really put in a lot of effort on that last writing assignment!"
"I think we did pretty well at staying focused and on-task during that last activity."	"How do you think we did at staying focused and on task during that last activity?"
"Tell me more about your idea."	"Share a bit more about your idea."

We all want students to feel ownership of their learning and their work, don't we? Learning is so much more authentic and purposeful when students feel a true sense of ownership. So, why do so many students rarely seem to take any real ownership of work? I think that it may have to do with the way we typically talk about work with students. Our language habits may indicate (as do the examples in the left column of Figure 9.1) that it is we, the teachers, who own the work, and it is the student's job to do our work. We may use teacher-centric language, explaining everything in the first-person, from our own perspective. We may accidentally keep redirecting class discussions back to ourselves.

If we want to help students feel more ownership of their work, let's consider a few simple language shifts that might help.

Shift from Teacher-Focused to Student-Focused Language

As teachers, we naturally think about what's going on in the classroom through our own perspectives. After all, we are the ones who craft units, plan lessons, and think about managing a class of diverse learners through complex tasks. We see the students, the classroom, and the learning through our own eyes. And yet, when we deliver instructions or make observations with our students, we need to be careful about how these messages come out. If we think aloud through our own lens, we may accidentally transmit the idea that school is all about us. When students do work for us, their sense of agency and power diminishes. Work becomes an exercise in compliance instead of engagement.

As you consider your language patterns through this lens, there are a couple of common habits to consider—ones that I have certainly fallen into myself and ones that I've seen many other teachers fall into as well. One of them is the overuse of the first person. Consider the difference between "I have an idea about how we can practice this writing skill" and "You're going to get to try a new way to practice this next writing skill."

Another common language habit that reinforces the idea that students are working for teachers (instead of themselves) is sliding in the phrase "for me" when describing what students will do or the work itself. Consider the following examples:

- "Here's the next thing you'll do for me in this music rehearsal."
- "Okay, everyone. Turn to page 35 for me, and we'll check out what's going to happen next in this story."
- "Jahmal, flip the next card over for me, and then read the challenge."

While each of these language habits may seem benign, consider their impact when they're repeated throughout the day, every day. Without meaning to, we may be giving hundreds of small messages to students that we own the work and that students are working for us instead of themselves. See Figure 9.2 for examples of how to shift these habits.

FIGURE 9.2

Instead of . . .	Try This . . .
"Hey, everyone. I was looking back through last week's assignments, and some of you still owe me some work."	"Hey, everyone. I was looking back through last week's assignments, and some of you still need to turn in some work."
"I've been thinking a lot about this next phase of our project, so here's what I've decided you're going to do."	"Here's your next step of the project."
"Be ready to show me what you've been trying."	"Be ready to share what you've been trying."
"Would someone raise your hand and show me what you have so far?"	"Would someone raise your hand and show what you have so far?"
"I would like for you to build a tower that is six cubic centimeters."	"Your next challenge is to build a tower that is six cubic centimeters."
"Try sounding out this word for me."	"Try sounding out this word."

What about, instead of using the singular "I" or "you" voice, we use the plural "we?" Teachers often ask me this question as we play with shifting from the first to second person, and it involves some nuance. For example, instead of saying, "Next up, I want you all to get out your reading books and meet in our circle area," we might say, "We're moving to reading now, so we all need to get our reading books and meet in our circle." This might work, depending on the situation. If it's legitimate to include yourself as a part of the group, then it probably works. "Let's all settle in for writing workshop so we can keep moving forward on our poetry anthology!" is probably an authentic use of the plural "let's." Everyone in the class, the teacher included, is working on the poetry anthology. "Let's all talk about how we struggled as a group yesterday during guided reading" may or may not feel authentic, and the deciding factor here will be tone. If the teacher genuinely feels a part of the group and is transmitting the idea that the whole group, the teacher included, owns the problem of the day before, this is probably appropriate. If, however, the teacher's tone indicates that he is really criticizing the group and that it's the students who are the problem, saying "We struggled as a class yesterday" (especially if in a high-pitched admonishing tone) might sound ironic and false.

Don't Thank Students Inappropriately

Just as we should avoid thanking students for positive behavior, we should be careful about thanking students for doing work. It can be tempting, though. "Thank you all so much for that great class discussion!" we might say, hoping to help students feel appreciated (and perhaps to especially appreciate those who participated a lot and encourage those who didn't to do so more in the future). But let's think about what we're really saying when we thank students for turning in their homework, participating in a discussion, or completing a project. This may be another subtle way that we accidentally send the message that students are working *for* us. "Thank you" implies that a favor has been done, or that the one doing the thanking is appreciative and has received some kind of benefit. In fact, what we want is for students to work for themselves—and to recognize that they are the ones receiving the benefit of completing work, trying hard, and participating.

So, instead of thanking students, we might celebrate with them, boosting their sense of accomplishment and helping them gain a deeper sense of ownership of their work. See Figure 9.3.

FIGURE 9.3

Instead of . . .	Try . . .
"Thanks so much, everyone, for putting in so much effort into that performance!"	"Wow! The effort you all put into the performance really paid off. The audience loved it!"
"Thank you for getting settled so quickly."	"It looks like you're ready to start."
"I appreciate the way you all engaged in a debate while still being respectful!"	"You were just able to engage in a debate while still being respectful—that can be hard to do, but you did it!"

Reinforce Students' High Expectations of Themselves

Extensive research has shown that teacher expectations of students have a clear effect on student achievement (Hattie, 2009, pp. 121–124). Just as important, we want our students to have high expectations of themselves. However, most of the time we speak about learning expectations from our own perspectives. When we say to students, "I'm going to be looking for really high-quality work in this next assignment," the message is clear. Students should be working to please us and should aim to meet our high expectations. Similarly, language that emphasizes grades (if teachers are the ones in control of grading) has the same effect. "In order to get an *A* on this next piece of work . . ." gives the clear message: "Do what I expect, and you'll get the good grade." Some teachers relish the idea of being a hard grader, which seems to even further reinforce that grades are about teacher-pleasing as opposed to meeting required learning standards.

What if, instead, we worked at transmitting the idea that it's students who should have high expectations for themselves? There are a couple of potentially key positive outcomes. First, the more we reinforce the assumption that students have high expectations for themselves, the more likely they are to feel and take on those expectations. Also, by constantly practicing this idea with our own language, we can start to shift our own mindsets, reinforcing the belief that students are intrinsically motivated and want to do great work! See Figure 9.4.

FIGURE 9.4	
Instead of . . .	**Try This . . .**
"I'm going to be looking for really high-quality writing in this next lab report. I want to see appropriate use of technical language, clean and correct formatting, and thorough and well-explained procedures and conclusions."	"There are a few key elements to work on in order to have high-quality writing in this next lab report. Look for the appropriate use of technical language, clean and correct formatting, and thorough and well-explained procedures and conclusions."
"I'd love to see some great effort during this next soccer practice."	"Some great effort during this practice will lead to results that you'll be proud of!"
"This paper doesn't work for me. You still haven't fully developed the argument, and the editing isn't complete. I want you to go clean it up!"	"This paper isn't finished yet. You still haven't fully developed the argument, and the editing isn't complete. It still needs some more work."

Boost Student Reflection

Another way we may accidentally retain too much control and ownership of learning is by oversharing our own thoughts and reflections about how things are going in the classroom. We finish a writing period and share with the class, "Wow! We just stayed focused and on-task for a solid 30 minutes. That was really productive!" Of course, there's nothing wrong with this statement. In fact, it is clear, specific, brief, and affirming, and it supports a positive learning environment. This kind of language is only problematic if it is *always* the teacher who does the reflecting and assessment of learning. If one of your goals is to increase student ownership of learning, you might consider passing off some of this reflection to students. See Figure 9.5.

FIGURE 9.5	
Instead of . . .	**Try This . . .**
"Wow! We just stayed focused and on-task for a solid 30 minutes. That was really productive!"	"Turn and talk with a partner: What did we just do to stay so focused and on-task as we wrote today?"
"On a scale of 1 to 5, I'd give that last activity a 4."	"On a scale of 1 to 5, how do you think we did on that last activity?"
"I think we were really struggling with working cooperatively in groups today."	"In your groups, share together: How did we do at working cooperatively today? What went well and what could have been better?"

Conclusion

A friend of mine is in a management position at a technology company in the Boston area. One of his greatest frustrations in his role as a manager is that several people he supports have a hard time thinking for themselves. He told me about one who was working on a project, got to a challenge, and immediately came to him, looking for an answer or a solution. "The problem with that is, I want her to think for herself. She needs to own the challenge and try something out. It's okay with me if the solution doesn't work. We'll learn from mistakes. But I need people in my work group to not rely on me for direction all of the time."

As our economy continues to shift, as more and more low-level jobs—ones that are linear and straightforward—are outsourced or automated, skills of self-motivation, self-management, and self-direction will become increasingly important. And it is nearly impossible

> **Other Ways to Boost Student Ownership**
>
> - Grade less and have students self-assess more.
>
> - Offer meaningful choices about what or how students learn.
>
> - Have students set relevant learning goals about work.
>
> - Brainstorm ideas as a class for how to practice skills or demonstrate learning.
>
> - Invite students to showcase work they're proud of on classroom or hallway walls.

for students to learn and practice these kinds of skills and work habits if they are in a system that continues to rely on compliance. Though the language shifts discussed in this chapter might seem subtle, the overall effect of creating learning environments where students feel true ownership of work is perhaps one of the most important shifts we can make in education today.

10

Increase Student Participation

When you're working with students, do you or your students do the majority of the talking? All too often, even in student-centered classrooms, teachers tend to talk way more than learners. In *Brilliance by Design* (2011), Vicki Halsey recommends a 70-30 principle: Learners should spend about 70 percent of the time talking and about 30 percent of the time listening. A little informal research that I conducted one day in a school confirmed my hunch that these numbers are usually reversed in schools.

One time I was working with a group of kindergarten and 1st grade teachers in New York City to consider strategies that would boost engagement and reduce disruptive behaviors that were getting in the way of learning. I spent a bit of time in each of their rooms throughout the day. As part of my observation work, I tracked the amount of time that teachers spent talking and the amount that students talked. Granted, this study was very informal. It was conducted on one day in one school. I checked my watch throughout each observation and jotted down quick estimates. Nonetheless, I think the results are telling. In these eight primary grade classrooms, teachers were talking about 65 percent of the time and students were talking about 35 percent of the time. This is not atypical, and if teachers are talking this much in primary grade classrooms, just imagine how much they talk in upper grades! In fact, according to many studies, students spend very little time engaged in actual discussion—anywhere from 1.7 minutes per hour to 0.5–3 percent of class time, depending on the study (Walsh & Sattes, 2015 p. 6).

It's good for us to remember the adage: "Whoever is doing the talking is doing the learning." Now, let's consider some ways we can make sure that our students are the ones doing most of the thinking!

Keep Mini-Lessons Mini: Maximize Student Work Time

I once heard a colleague say that there are three moments in any lesson: The *golden moment* is whatever you say in the first 60 seconds. The *silver moment* is whatever you say in the last 60 seconds. The *leaden moment* is everything in between. A bit extreme perhaps, but the point is worth considering. There's a reason that TED talks have a 20-minute time limit. There's just so long that the human brain can attend to direct instruction.

Lessons should be short and sweet. Keep teaching points to a minimum, and give students lots of time to process, consolidate, and extend learning through partner or small-group discussions, activities, and other active and interactive structures. If you're teaching a longer lesson through direct lecture, consider breaking it up into smaller bite-size parts. In his book *Brain Rules* (2014), developmental molecular biologist and professor John Medina suggests what he calls the "10-minute rule" when giving lectures. In this teaching model for keeping longer lectures engaging, he recommends breaking longer talks up into 10-minute sections, with each section focusing on one core concept. At the end of each 10-minute block, the teacher should give the audience a break from information and switch to a brief relevant story or some other hook to allow listeners to regain their attention and be ready to listen to more content.

A common teacher practice that unnecessarily lengthens lessons is the Q&A format as a method for direct instruction. This is when a teacher, in a well-intentioned effort to involve and engage students, "teaches" content by asking students questions. Let's compare the opening of a lesson done this way to a more direct style of instruction in Figure 10.1.

FIGURE 10.1	
Instead of a Q&A Lesson . . .	**Try Direct Instruction . . .**
Teacher: Today we're going to practice multiplication. Who can remember one of the strategies we've used? Student 1: Lattice? Teacher: Yes! Who remember how to do that one? Student 2: Well, first you have to make a rectangle and write the numbers on the sides. Teacher: Maybe. Are you thinking of lattice multiplication or another one like using open arrays? Student 2: I don't know. Teacher: Okay, so I'll draw a rectangle and put numbers on the side. Who knows what comes next? Student 3: You have to draw diagonal lines. But I don't like this one. I prefer to use partial products. Teacher: Okay, but right now we're showing lattice. So, yeah, you draw diagonal lines—like this. Now what? Student 2: Like I said before, you write the numbers on the side—put them on the insides. Teacher: Okay. I see what you mean. I'll write the numbers in, but actually, they go on the outside. What's next? Student 4: I've already got the answer. It's 1,036. Teacher: Okay, but what did you do next to solve it?	Teacher: Today we're going to practice multiplication. You can use any of the strategies we've worked on so far. I'm going to give a brief demonstration of each, just to jog your memory. In the lattice method, you draw a rectangle with diagonal lines, like this. Remember to line the factors on the outside of the rectangle, and then multiply inside the boxes—like this.

There are a couple of key problems with the Q&A style of lesson. First off, it's confusing. In addition to some correct information, students also hear each other's approximations, misinformation, or tangential comments. According to a meta-analysis of studies exploring the correlation between teacher clarity of communication and student achievement, teachers' ability to communicate clearly in an interesting and well-paced manner had a significant impact on student learning (Fendick, 1990). The Q&A style of teaching lessons is anything but clear, interesting, or well-paced and can lead some students who worry they don't know the right answers to feel diminished, making them more reluctant to participate.

It's also inefficient. Lessons delivered in this style can take more than twice as long as ones delivered more directly. This can lead students with short attention spans to get bored and either tune out or become disruptive, which further inhibits learning for all. The same is true for students who already know the content—they quickly disengage as lessons ramble. What could have been a crisp 5-minute mini-lesson becomes a 25-minute slog, with some students melting down and everyone losing valuable time to work.

Reduce Echo Talk

Another common language habit that tends to swing the ratio of teacher to student talk toward the teacher is *echo talk*. This is when a teacher echoes back what students say (see the sidebar for an example). In addition to increasing the amount of teacher talk in the room, this habit sends the message that the students don't need to listen to each other. It may even hint that if the teacher doesn't say something, it doesn't count.

As I work with teachers on this language habit, some common reasons for using echo talk arise. For some, it's an unconscious pattern. For many however, it's an intentional strategy. They echo to reinforce or validate students' ideas. We need to ask ourselves—do we want students to think that ideas are valid only if we say them? Instead, we might acknowledge students' contributions by nodding or smiling without talking. Or, invite them to extend their thinking: "Tell more about that

> ### Example of Echo Talk
>
> Teacher: What do you think Bilbo might do next in *The Hobbit?*
>
> Student: He might run away.
>
> Teacher (nodding): He might run away. Who else has an idea?
>
> Student: He might try to kill Gollum.
>
> Teacher: Mm-hm. He might try to kill Gollum. Who else?
>
> Student: He could try and find the dwarves.
>
> Teacher: He could try and find the dwarves.

idea." Some teachers echo because they're worried that students can't hear each other. If this is the case, teach students to speak more clearly and to ask each other to repeat themselves when needed. In some classrooms, students have a signal they use (such as a hand to their ear) if they can't hear a classmate.

Avoid the Rhetorical "Right?"

A relatively new speech habit that I've noticed creeping into classrooms (and the general lexicon, for that matter) is what I call the *rhetorical "right?"* I've caught myself using it a few times and I'm working at nipping this in the bud before it becomes a new habit. It sounds something like this: "So, clearly, Lincoln wanted to preserve the Union at all costs, right? He also wanted to abolish slavery, but he knew his primary duty as president was to try and keep the country together, right?"

Sliding in the question "right?" at the end of a statement offers the illusion of student participation, but it's not really meant to be answered. Instead, it offers the speaker a false sense of agreement and attention on the part of the audience. It says, "I've said something, and you agree, so we can keep moving along." When I've heard myself use this phrase, I've noticed that it feels good—like you're getting agreement from someone.

Another similar language habit is asking the class a question such as, "Do you mind if I skip ahead to the next point?" Again, this feels participatory, as if the teacher is seeking student input into the direction of a lesson. While students may nod or voice that it's okay, do they really have an option here? These language habits might lead a teacher to feel as though there is actual class participation, when, in fact, students aren't saying anything.

Ask More Open-Ended Questions

Too often in schools, questions typically elicit fairly low-level responses. This style of questioning, which Walsh and Sattes refer to as IRE, follows a predictable pattern: Initiate, Respond, Evaluate (2015, p. 7). The teacher asks a question for which there is one right answer. A student answers the question. Then the teacher evaluates the answer—usually as either right or wrong. In addition to keeping classroom discourse fairly rote, this style also keeps the possession of learning squarely in the court of the teacher. Just consider the ratio of this structure—2:1 in favor of the teacher.

Instead, we could work at using more open-ended questions. Open-ended questions elicit a wider variety of possible acceptable responses and are by far more interesting and thought-provoking for students. They're also more inclusive, inviting students with many different ideas to share, not just the ones who know the "right" answer. Finally, these questions increase student talk because many students may share ideas about each question (see Figure 10.2).

FIGURE 10.2

Closed Questions	Open-Ended Questions
"How many sides does a rectangle have?"	"What are some examples of rectangles that you see in our classroom?"
"At what temperature does water freeze?"	"What are some different types of frozen precipitation?"
"What is impressionism?"	"What are some characteristics of impressionism that you enjoy?"

Use Interactive Discussion Structures

A fantastic way to boost the power of open-ended questions and increase the time students spend answering them is through interactive discussion structures. These learning structures allow all students to talk instead of just one at a time, as is often the case in traditional class "discussions." In addition to helping boost the amount of talking that students do, these structures can also, to a degree, equalize student talk. While it can be easy for a few students to dominate in a whole-class discussion, more students get to have an equal voice in partner chats or small-group discussions.

A Few Interactive Discussion Structures

- **Mix and Mingle to the Music:** As music is played, students mix and mingle. When the music stops, everyone joins with a nearby partner for a brief discussion.
- **Card Match:** Students receive cards (playing cards, vocab words, synonyms, etc.) and find their match for a chat. Shuffle cards and repeat.
- **Commonalities:** Name a category (color of clothing, letters in your name, etc.). Students find a partner or small group who have that in common and engage in a brief discussion.

Though a turn-and-talk is a simple and common interactive discussion structure, there are dozens more to consider. Many of these structures have the added benefit of getting students up and moving, fueling the brain with oxygen, boosting energy and students' ability to think and converse well. Though they require a bit more explicit management than class discussions where everyone sits still and listens to one person at a time speak, the benefits are well worth the extra effort.

These structures can be used to give students time to consolidate learning during a lesson, brainstorm ideas, prepare for a discussion, or for any number of other purposes. There are many great resources out there to give you more ideas. You might start with Persida and William Himmele's *Total Participation Techniques* (2017). It's packed with tons of practical strategies for helping students take a more active role in their learning.

Conclusion

It might seem surprising that in a book all about teacher talk, there would be an entire chapter devoted to talking less. But sometimes, we just need to be quiet and let the students do the thinking!

Boost Intrinsic Motivation

"Kids these days just aren't motivated!" we might hear an elementary school teacher say. "They just want to fool around or play video games."

"My students just don't care. They just want to do the least amount possible and finish as fast as they can so they can talk with their friends," we might hear a middle school colleague complain.

Perhaps you've heard a high school teacher worry about his or her students: "All my students care about is grades. I want them to be passionate about learning, but they just want me to give them a rubric and tell them what to do."

Don't we all want our students to be motivated to learn? More specifically, don't we want our students to be motivated from within—to have a hunger and drive for learning that compels them to work hard and engage in robust challenges? Yet so often, students seem so passive. They either resist learning or slide by with minimal effort, doing the least amount possible. This entire book connects with motivation in some ways, but in this chapter we'll address the topic head-on. We'll explore ways to boost intrinsic motivation (motivation that comes from within) in our students. Before we get to this though, we must first understand what we're up against, so we will explore extrinsic motivation—the primary form of motivation offered to students in school.

Extrinsic motivators (prizes, treats, monetary rewards, food, etc.) compel us to do things we might not otherwise want to do with the promise of prospective gain. Students get stickers for bringing in their homework, shallow praise ("Good job!") for walking quietly in the hall, student-of-the-week awards for being responsible, pizza for reading a certain number of books, and good grades for compliant work.

When my daughter, Carly, was in elementary school, she had a teacher who was working hard to motivate kids to do well. She used a reward system where the class collected warm-fuzzies (mini pom-pom balls) in a jar by following rules and getting compliments from other teachers. When the jar was full, they got their reward: a goof-off day. The teacher explained that kids could wear pajamas to school and didn't have to do any work all day long. When explaining this to parents, she winked and said, "But actually, we're playing math and literacy games all day long. They have so much fun, they don't even know they're learning!"

Although this teacher would say that she believes that learning is and should be fun, by rewarding students with a goof-off day, she actually sent the reverse message. If the reward is to not do work, work must be something inherently distasteful—something to avoid if you can. Similarly, when she explains that kids are having so much fun they don't even know they're learning, she's revealing her belief that learning isn't fun. If students somehow knew they were learning, the logic goes, it would decrease the pleasure of the moment.

There are many problems with relying on extrinsic motivators in school. Study after study after study reveals that the use of extrinsic motivators decreases intrinsic motivation. Here's one: A group of preschoolers were gathered. All of these children already loved to draw. Then, some of them were offered rewards for drawing, some were surprised with unexpected rewards, and others were given no reward at all. Students who were offered the reward ahead of time (meaning their behavior was incentivized) showed a dramatic decrease in their desire to draw after the study was done (Lepper, Greene, & Nisbett, 1973).

In a meta-analysis of 128 studies on the effect of extrinsic rewards on intrinsic motivation, researchers concluded that rewards, whether they are offered for engagement, completion of a task, or performance, all significantly undermined intrinsic motivation (Deci, Koestner, & Ryan, 1999). So, when we offer pizza for kids who read over the summer, we may increase the number of books that kids read that summer, but we likely decrease their intrinsic drive to read in general. When we give preschoolers a sticker for singing a song, we dampen their joy of singing. When we give a class a "goof-off day" for working hard and being kind, we make them less likely to want to work hard or be kind on their own. When we offer kids As for learning, we diminish their intrinsic motivation to learn.

Extrinsic motivators also decrease achievement. In a series of fascinating studies, Edward Deci, a psychologist at the University of Rochester, and his colleagues found time and time again that when both elementary school children and college students were asked to learn information to take a test, they learned less than students who simply read the content (without the knowledge of an upcoming test) or those who learned content to teach others (Deci et al., 1999, pp. 47–48). Remember those preschoolers who lost their interest in drawing after being incentivized? Judges also rated their pictures as less aesthetically pleasing than the drawings of the non-incentivized students.

As noted in Chapter 7, another problem with incentives and rewards is that these extrinsic motivators may encourage students to view work as optional because it's now transactional. Just think—if students are told, "Do this assignment and you'll get a sticker," they may now start weighing their options: "Is doing that work worth a sticker?" They may conclude that it isn't and choose not to do the work. I've heard teachers exclaim in exasperation about a student who won't turn in work, "They're getting Fs and they don't even care!" Right! Working for grades isn't sufficiently motivational, and they've decided that their time and effort isn't worth the grade. Mark Twain deftly pointed out this phenomenon in *The Adventures of Tom Sawyer* (1876), at the end of the glorious whitewasher scene: "There are wealthy gentlemen in England who drive four-horse passenger-coaches twenty or thirty miles on a daily line, in the summer, because the privilege costs them considerable money; but if they were offered wages for the service, that would turn it into work and then they would resign."

We've all had students who seem to not care about their work. Some students show this by disconnecting entirely—not doing work and failing classes. Others show it by complying and doing the bare minimum. "Just give me the rubric so I know what I have to do to get a *B*," they say. What's sad is that kids don't come to school like this. Have you ever seen an unmotivated 4-year-old? Remember those fired up learners in Kathy Bresciano's and Suzanne Ryan's classrooms, described at the beginning of Chapter 8? They show up for preschool ready to go! They want to paint, build, act, look at books, experiment in the sand table, and sing. I think it's pretty clear that the system of rewards and incentives that is so pervasive in schools is a leading contributor to students' diminished intrinsic motivation as they move through school. Stickers, candy, prizes, grades, and even hollow praise slowly undermine students' passion for learning.

Eliminating all such devices from our schools, especially structures like grades and schoolwide awards, takes a massive amount of time and effort and goes way beyond the scope of this book (though it would be a worthy cause!). What we can do is change the way we talk about learning, work, and behavior. So, let's focus on language. How can we, while still navigating (and helping our students navigate) the structures of our schools, emphasize intrinsic motivation through our language?

What Are Intrinsic Motivators?

First, we need to know what intrinsic motivation is all about. Extrinsic motivation is so common in schools that we may, at first, struggle to figure out what intrinsic motivation should look like. If kids aren't working for grades, treats, or prizes, what should motivate them? This may be especially hard to answer for those who grew up being motivated with extrinsic motivators. If praise, grades, and stickers are all we've experienced as ways to motivate our learning, the idea that motivation can come from within might be hard to grasp at first.

Intrinsic motivators are ones that compel us from within—they're qualities that make something worthy of action on its own. For example, you might knit in the evening because it helps you relax and you enjoy the accomplishment of completing a new project. You might sing in a choir for the joy of music and the comradery of the group. You might volunteer at a local charity or civic organization for a sense of purpose: It feels good to help your neighbors and community. There are many different intrinsic motivators, but most of them fit into one of a few broad categories. The following list is drawn from multiple sources including Maslow's hierarchy of needs, Glasser's choice theory, the work of Edward Deci in *Why We Do What We Do* (1995), and essential elements of self-motivation outlined by Daniel Pink in *Drive: The Surprising Truth About What Motivates Us* (2009).

> **A Few Strategies That Tap into Intrinsic Motivation (In Addition to Language)**
>
> • Working with partners or in small groups
>
> • Having authentic choices about learning
>
> • Playing (and creating!) games to deepen learning
>
> • Employing student goal-setting and self-assessment strategies
>
> • Doing real work: writing books, giving presentations to a real audience, publishing a website, community service learning

- **Belonging:** We long for social connection. It feels good to be part of a group and have friends.
- **Autonomy:** We want to be self-directed—to have some power and control over what we do and how we do it.
- **Mastery:** It feels good to grow and learn—to gain a sense of mastery. We relish challenges when we perceive they are within our reach.
- **Significance:** We want our work to matter—to have some greater purpose beyond the moment or ourselves.
- **Fun:** We all crave a sense of fun and enjoyment. We want to be positively engaged.

The good news is, if the work we're doing with students is valuable and interesting, it's going to have some of these qualities inherently built into it. For example, it's exciting for students to see themselves getting better as readers and writers (mastery/esteem). When we give students choices about their work, we are sharing autonomy and power with them. When students know they will be sharing their writing or their research findings with others, or if they will perform in front of an audience, we can tap into their desire for purpose, belonging, and significance. In the following sections, notice these and other themes that run through many of the examples. They may help you consider how to talk about student work and learning in ways that align with what is (or should be!) intrinsically motivating about work.

Assume and Emphasize Intrinsic Motivation

As I talk with students and ask them about language habits and patterns of their teachers, I'm surprised at how many share experiences with teachers who talk about work being unpleasant or boring. "I know some of you don't love history," a teacher might say while introducing the next social studies unit. "This next worksheet is kind of boring, but it has some important ideas," explains a Spanish teacher as he introduces the next skill students will be practicing. One student told me that his Algebra teacher actually began a math lesson by saying, "I don't want to do this any more than you do, but it's on the state test, so we have to." Just think of the tone this sets in a classroom! If we wanted to create apathetic unmotivated students, these statements would be a great place to start.

Instead, let's use language that assumes that students are already motivated and emphasizes characteristics of the work that are intrinsically motivating. See Figure 11.1.

FIGURE 11.1	
Instead of . . .	**Try This . . .**
"In this next activity, find a problem to work on. For those of you who get nervous about pushing yourself, don't worry, there should be one there that won't be too hard."	"In this next activity, find a puzzle or problem that will be exciting to work on—one that will get your wheels turning."
"I know you guys just want to get to your books, but first I have to teach a quick mini-lesson."	"We're going to be talking about a new reading strategy today—one that will help you understand important ideas in your reading."
"I know some of you don't love singing, but this next song is actually kind of good."	"This next song is fascinating. You're going to be amazed at the story it tells!"

Use Appropriately Challenging Vocabulary

A way to tap into students' need for mastery is to use (and encourage students to use) challenging and technical terminology. Gaining mastery of new words gives students a sense of power and strength. This might be vocabulary related to a content area. For example, students learning music can enjoy gaining mastery of words such as *forte*, *pianissimo*, and *andantino*. Or, we might introduce students to words related to the process of learning. Young students love trying out terms like *metacognition* and *character analysis*. When I introduced 5th graders to the idea of multiple intelligences (Gardner, 2011) as a way to generate ideas for projects they might create to share their research with classmates, many of them delighted in using terms such as *interpersonal*, *linguistic*, and *intrapersonal*.

In their book, *Learning and Leading with Habits of Mind* (2008), Art Costa and Bena Kallick encourage teachers to use "mindful" language with students as a way to "enhance students' awareness and performance of these intelligent behaviors" (p. 124). In fact, they point out that students are more likely to adopt these habits of mind when teachers use specific, cognitive terminology. For example, they suggest that instead of saying, "Let's look at these two pictures," we might try, "Let's compare these two pictures." Using words like *hypothesize*, *evaluate*, *apply*, and *speculate* will not only boost students' excitement for learning but will also help them internalize the words and use the skills (pp. 124–125).

Emphasize Immediate Motivators
(and Avoid "You'll Need This Someday")

A common fallback we might use, especially when we can't identify other intrinsic motivators in work students are doing, is to say some version of, "This is important because you'll need it later." Emphasizing the importance of math fact fluency, we might say, "Next year in 5th grade, teachers are going to expect you to multiply quickly." Or, if a student asks us, "When am I going to need to know how to write up a science report?" we might respond with, "If you end up going into science, you'll need to know how to do this." Of course, there are a couple of problems with relying on "someday" as students' primary motivation. First, people are notoriously bad at doing hard things now for possible gains later on. It's hard for us to save for retirement, force ourselves to exercise, or eat well. I'm not saying it's not a worthy cause to help kids get better at delaying gratification—quite the contrary. I just don't think it's a good way to build positive energy for practicing math facts in the moment. Second, because "someday" is fictional (we don't really know what tomorrow holds, let alone what may happen 10 years from now), it's easy to dismiss and argue away: "I don't plan on being a scientist, so I guess I don't care about writing a lab report" or "I can multiply on my phone, so I don't need to practice multiplication."

A teacher I worked with in Todd County High School in Mission, South Dakota, warns of another version of "You'll need it someday." He cautions us to stop using the phrase "in the real world," and I couldn't agree more. You know what he means: "In the real world, people are going to expect you to be able to work well with others, so you'd better figure this out now." This language habit is problematic for a couple of reasons. Like "you'll need this someday," it can be a weak substitute for better, more immediate intrinsic motivators. It's also dismissive of students' current lives and situations. It's almost like we're saying that where they are right now—both in school and at home—isn't real life.

Instead, we should work at connecting with more immediate intrinsic motivators. Writing a lab report that will be shared with another class or published online (instead of just being turned in for a grade) builds a sense of purpose. Playing a game to practice math fact fluency is fun in the moment. We should always look for ways to connect with intrinsic motivators so that we don't need to incentivize learning.

Reduce Teacher-Pleasing Language

One of the most common forms of extrinsic language used in schools is teacher-pleasing language—the same kind we discussed in Chapter 7 when exploring how language influences moral reasoning. This habit of talk emphasizes that the reason for doing work is to make a teacher happy or comply with the wishes of a teacher. You might be thinking, isn't belonging an intrinsic motivator? Don't we want students to have strong connections with and please teachers? Yes, but there's a difference between building connections with students and having them dependent on us for approval.

First, let's remember that students are already yearning for positive connections with teachers—even the students who seem sullen and disconnected. (These students have learned that it's safer to be angry than vulnerable.) When we smile and nod as we listen to a student during a writing conference, when we ask a follow-up question after a student has asked for help, when we build connections with students by sharing about ourselves and learning about them, we are helping them meet their needs for belonging and connection.

It's when we use that connection as a reason for doing something else that the language shifts to a form of extrinsic motivation. In Chapter 8, we considered how this affects behavior. Now, let's consider academic engagement and motivation. "I like the way you got so many sources for your research project!" indicates that the reason students should get lots of resources is because we like it. Our approval is now the incentive or reward for doing good work. We can shift this language to emphasize purpose and mastery: "You have quite a few sources for your research project. That lends a lot of credibility to your work—showing that you thought deeply about the topic. It also helps give multiple perspectives to some of your research questions!" See Figure 11.2 for a few more examples.

FIGURE 11.2

Instead of Emphasizing Approval . . .	Try Tapping into Intrinsic Motivators . . .
"Jayson, I love the way you're working so hard on your clay model!"	"Jayson, your hard work is really paying off. Your model has realistic detail!"
"I'm so happy with how that last artist-writers workshop went!"	"Did you see how great that last work period was? We got a lot of writing and artwork prepared for our upcoming exhibit!"
"Wow! I like how you wrote such a long story, Hannah!"	"Hannah, that might be the longest story you've written yet. Congratulations!"

This doesn't mean that we should completely remove ourselves from the equation, however. In Chapter 9, I suggest shifting from first person to second person language as one way to emphasize student ownership of language. You may have noticed this trend in the previous chart. This is a good habit to consider, but there are certainly times when it might be appropriate to use the first person. Perhaps the class is having a discussion, and you want to share your opinion as a member of the class. "Here's a thought I have," you might begin. Or, perhaps you're responding to a student's writing and want to speak from the perspective of a reader: "As a reader, I was struck by the imagery you used in this opening paragraph." In each of these instances, you are placing yourself on a level playing field with students. You are a class member offering an idea, or you are a reader responding as a reader. By reducing the hierarchy of positions, we are able to use the first-person voice in a way that's less likely to be interpreted by students as a voice of power.

Shift the Way We Talk About Tests and Grades

Surprise! It's time for a pop quiz.

1. Which of the following statements best reflects the role that tests and quizzes should play in student learning?
    a. Students should learn so they can do well on tests and quizzes.
    b. Tests and quizzes are one way we can understand student learning.
2. Which of the following statements best reflects the role that grades should play in student learning?
    a. Grades are a reward for learning.
    b. Grades should reflect student learning.

If you answered "b" to each of these pop quiz questions, then you likely don't see tests and quizzes or grades as the primary motivator for learning. In my experience, most educators want to respond "b." We want learning, not tests and grades, to be the goal, yet we may find ourselves accidentally communicating the reverse to students through our language. "To get an *A*, you should study" implies that the reason for studying is to get a good grade. The tail wags the dog. Instead, tap into an intrinsic motivator by connecting with students' need for mastery and competence: "To master this material, you should study." Does this mean that making this shift will suddenly cause all students to study? Of course not. But think about the message it sends. The goal of studying is learning and mastery. Even if it doesn't shift behavior immediately, it better reflects the kind of intrinsic motivation that we want to help foster in our students (see Figure 11.3).

FIGURE 11.3

Instead of . . .	Try This . . .
"If you want to do well on tomorrow's quiz, you'd better study!"	"Studying will help you master the concepts we've been working on. Tomorrow's quiz will help us check in to see how things are going."
"This rubric will help make sure you know how to get an *A*."	"This rubric will help you push yourself to do great work."
"I know some of you are trying to get your grades up right now, so make sure you work really hard on this next unit."	"I know some of you have been working hard to understand the content in the last two units. Make sure to work hard in this next unit."
"If you're not happy with your grade, you can make some revisions and submit your essay again next Tuesday."	"If you want to continue to improve your essay, you can make some revisions and submit it again next Tuesday."

Conclusion

One challenge for us as teachers, as we consider ways to tap into intrinsic motivation in daily learning, is that we ourselves likely grew up in a school environment that emphasized compliance. "Why do I have to show my work, if I know the answer?" we might have asked in math class. We likely heard the reply, "Because that's what you're supposed to do. You have to show your work." For many of us, school has always been about compliance, and now that we find ourselves at the front of the room, we may end up in the same system. For example, if we're struggling to implement curricula that others have developed, and we ask the curriculum coordinator, "Why do I need to teach that lesson if my kids didn't get the last one?" we may hear a response that's eerily familiar: "Because that's what you're supposed to do. It's about fidelity to the program."

If we can't even determine what should be intrinsically motivating about students' (or our) work, how can we use language habits that emphasize intrinsic motivation?

We'll get into many specific strategies for shifting language habits in Chapter 14, but here's an idea to try right away. Look at some of the lessons and units that you teach through the lens of the five intrinsic motivators listed in this chapter: belonging, autonomy, mastery, significance, and fun. As you think about the work, what intrinsic motivators are already present? For example, will students share their work on a bulletin board, through an online forum, or in a presentation? If so, that connects with a sense of significance. Will students have some choice about what they're learning or how they're learning it? If so, that may boost their sense of autonomy. Do students get to work with a partner (belonging) or play a game (fun) or chart their progress toward a goal (mastery)? Once you have identified the intrinsic motivators, you can now start to think about how to emphasize those as you talk with students about the work. And what if you can't find any intrinsic motivators? Then you can think about how you can shift the work so that it connects with at least one. Find ways of connecting whatever work students do with at least one intrinsic motivator, and your students will have a chance to move from being compliant to being more truly engaged in their learning.

There's an important benefit here that at least needs to be mentioned. When students are truly motivated about their school work, when it taps into their intrinsic drives, there will be fewer misbehaviors in your class. Too often, schools tackle discipline challenges without looking to the qualities of the academic work students are doing, and this is a huge mistake. It's almost impossible for many students to display positive behavior in the midst of work that's not motivating.

12

Focus on Growth and Learning

Few ideas have made such a splash on the education landscape as Carol Dweck's work on mindsets. Although Dweck, a researcher and professor of psychology at Stanford University, had been researching and publishing studies about developing a growth mindset for decades, it wasn't until her groundbreaking book *Mindset* was published in 2006 that many educators became familiar with her research. The thorough and celebrated work of Angela Duckworth (2016) in the field of psychology aligns nicely with Dweck's. Duckworth's research on grit (summarized in a compelling book of that title) makes the strong case that effort and hard work are far more important than talent when it comes to achievement and success.

Dweck's message is so compelling: The way we talk about learning is the key. When we praise students for their abilities and talents ("You're so smart!" "You're such a great writer!" "You're a fantastic artist!"), we reinforce the idea that talent or intelligence is fixed and that it's the key to success. Instead, we should focus on praising students for their effort, to help them understand the importance and value of hard work in success. Yet, as we've already seen in this book, it's not as simple as moving from "You're such a great writer" to "I love how hard you're working in writing." So, let's explore a few language strategies that will help students develop a growth mindset so they are willing to put in the hard work and effort needed to gain success. In this section, we will think not just about the oral language we use but also the written feedback we use to support student growth and learning.

Model a Growth Mindset

I've said it before, and I'll say it again: Great teachers are master learners. After all, how could we facilitate great learning if we aren't learners ourselves? It's important for students to see this part of who we are. We need to make sure to be clear with students about how we learn, including when we struggle and when we're taking risks.

A strategy suggested in Chapter 8 (sharing stories of engaged learning) comes in handy again. We might share stories of our own learning experiences that are directly related to the content we're teaching. For example, when teaching a unit on poetry in a writing workshop, we might say, "When I was a kid, I struggled to connect with poetry. I was caught up in trying to make everything rhyme. Then, I took a summer course that helped me see poetry in a new light. I've really enjoyed playing around with some new kinds of poetry and see myself getting better!"

We might also share stories of our own growth and learning that aren't directly related to the content we teach. We can slide them in during lessons to emphasize a key point or even share them on the side when we have a few moments as we chat with students. We might share a story of how we learned to drive or how we practiced a sport. We might share a current hobby that we're exploring.

Another way to model a growth mindset is to let students know when you're trying something new or taking a risk as a teacher: "We're going to do an activity today that I've never tried with a class before. I'm not sure how it's going to turn out!" Or, we might share a goal that we have as a teacher and invite students to help us learn and grow: "This year, one of my goals is to keep learning active and interactive. Would you all help me think about how I'm doing with that? If you've been sitting and listening for a while and feel like you need to move, let me know!"

What's important is that we help students see the adults who surround them in schools as learners—people who are constantly working toward goals, struggling with new challenges, and enjoying the struggle. At the front door to the elementary school where I first taught, there was a quote by Eric Hoffer printed on a bright yellow background: "In times of change, learners will inherit the earth, while the learned will find themselves beautifully equipped to deal with a world that no longer exists."

Be Thoughtful When Using Self-Deprecating Humor

How often do you hear teachers being overly self-critical and self-deprecating, modeling negative self-talk and a fixed mindset? "Ugh. I can't draw my way out of a paper bag," a teacher might exclaim, trying to sketch a map on a dry-erase board. "I don't have a musical bone in my body," laments another as he talks with his students about the upcoming band concert.

We might even say these kinds of things intentionally. After all, a well-placed joke at our own expense can help lighten a mood and reinforce the idea that teachers aren't good at everything and are still learners. So, if you use self-deprecating humor, I'd encourage you to do so in a way that models a growth mindset ("I try not to scare people with my singing. I can't even imagine the amount of practice it would take for me to carry a tune!"). I'd also encourage you to use this humor sparingly, so it doesn't become the tone of the room or the ongoing narrative of yourself as a learner. If we want students to see teachers as model learners, we should be thoughtful and purposeful about the way we talk about our own learning (see Figure 12.1).

FIGURE 12.1	
Instead of . . .	**Try This . . .**
"I've never be able to play the piano. I just don't have the music gene."	"Playing the piano is a skill I haven't practiced a lot."
"I'm not creative. I've never been good at writing fiction."	"I've really worked at nonfiction writing. Fiction, on the other hand, is something I don't have a lot of practice with."
"I've never had a head for memorizing. I always have to look things up."	"Memorization is an area I could use some work on. Fortunately, I can always look up information when I need it!"

Offer Descriptive, Specific Feedback

Kim Scott is the author of *Radical Candor: Be a Kick-Ass Boss Without Losing Your Humanity.* Russ Laraway is a career-long operational manager across the Marines, Google, and Twitter. Together, they cohost a podcast called "Radical Candor." Though the podcast's target audience is people in management positions in companies, there is a lot of potential transfer to the world of teaching and much overlap with the work of Carol Dweck. After all, part of teachers' work is to manage and support learners in their growth in much the same way that managers in businesses should nurture and support their employees. In multiple episodes of their podcast, Scott and Laraway address the issue of giving effective feedback. In addition to emphasizing the importance of building positive relationships for feedback to work well, they have some powerful insights into the nature and purpose of good feedback. They explain that people sometimes think that feedback is supposed to be about making people feel a certain way: Praise should make people feel good, and criticism should make people feel bad. This isn't actually the case. They contend that both praise and criticism are about helping people be more successful. Positive feedback should help people understand what they did well so they can build on it. Criticism should help people learn from mistakes so they can grow. In the podcast episode titled "Radically Candid Criticism" Scott advises, "Be really specific about what was great or be really clear about what it is that needs improvement."

Feedback is critical to learning. It helps students understand how they're doing in relation to goals and learning targets, and when done well, can support students' intrinsic drive to master content and enjoy learning. Feedback that emphasizes personal approval or evaluation (such as "Great job") is rarely helpful because

A Few Learner-Centric Alternatives to "Good Job"

- "You did it!"
- "Congratulations!"
- "That was a tough one!"
- "You nailed it."
- "You worked hard on that one!"
- "Yep. That's just right."

it doesn't give information about learning and tends to result in students avoiding the risks inherent in a challenging task (Hattie, 2009, p. 177).

Effective feedback should be descriptive instead of judgmental and help students better understand their progress toward goals. When we offer students concrete observations about their work, skills, or growth, we help strengthen their sense of competence and reinforce their intrinsic drive to master content. This requires a shift for teachers, though, especially if we are used to judging students (see Figure 12.2). It means that we must be master observers who are intent on picking up details of students' work to share. It means that we share less of what we think or feel and more of what

FIGURE 12.2

Instead of . . .	Try This . . .
"Great reading!"	"You read that part of the story with expression, and you made the characters sound like they were really talking!"
"I like your drawing!"	"The way you shaded this one part of the drawing gives the picture depth and power."
"Needs work."	"The last few paragraphs seemed rushed. Try reworking those and adding some more detail."
"That's *A+* work."	"The time and attention you spent on that project really paid off. It is neat, organized, and polished. Congratulations!"

we see. It means that we move away from being a judge and jury and slide into the role of coach.

Let's also continue to keep in mind other characteristics of effective feedback that have already been discussed in other sections of this book. We might move away from teacher-pleasing or teacher-centric language. For example, instead of saying, "I love the way you used multiple problem-solving strategies to tackle that task," we might say, "You used multiple problem-solving strategies to tackle that task!" Or, we might encourage students to self-reflect: "You used multiple problem-solving techniques to tackle that task. Which ones seemed especially helpful?"

Focus Feedback on Effort and Attributes, Not Talent

When we emphasize intelligence or talent when giving students feedback about their work, we run the risk of putting them into a fixed mindset, which makes them much less likely to take on challenges or risks in their learning. So, clearly, we need to make sure our feedback to students focuses on effort. As you look at the following examples, consider how in addition to emphasizing effort over talent, there's another characteristic at work. Each one tries to elicit some thinking about what students did or what attributes are strong about their work. This can help them better understand the skills or characteristics at work, enabling them to build on their successes (see Figure 12.3).

FIGURE 12.3	
Instead of . . .	**Try This . . .**
"You're such a great writer!"	"Your work on that last story really shows. The plot is well developed, and the characters are interesting!"
"You're such a gifted mathematician!"	"You must really enjoy mathematics. I bet you work hard at it!"
"Oh, I wish I had your kind of artistic talent."	"How have you developed such skills as an artist? Have you spent a lot of time drawing and painting?"
"Try harder."	"Some more time and attention are needed in the introduction of your report. Make sure to clearly describe and define the problem that you were working on."

Carol Dweck also cautions against the oversimplification of her research and advice. It's way too easy to substitute "Great job!" with "Great try!" and think this signifies a switch to growth mindset language (Dweck, 2016). In fact, this is still shallow praise, which can do more harm than good. A review of research suggests that this kind of language is especially likely to backfire when used with adolescents, making them less likely to believe that they can improve their intelligence or skills through hard work (Amemiya & Wang, 2018). Dweck also warns of telling students that they can accomplish anything through effort. "Just work hard, and you can accomplish anything!" is simply hollow encouragement if that's all that is offered to children struggling with a challenge. They need more specific guidance and coaching for hard work and effort to truly pay dividends.

Reconsider How to Encourage Hard Work

Because we value hard work and effort, we often encourage students to work hard and try hard. This makes sense, and it's important. However, we should think about the way we do this. We may unintentionally demotivate if we encourage hard work in certain ways. Here are a few we should watch out for.

"Try Your Best."

A few years ago, I was trying to break a goal time I'd set for myself as a runner, and I had one last 5K road race of the season before winter arrived. I had trained hard, had rested, and had the right pre-race spaghetti dinner the night before. The race was tough and hillier than I had anticipated. I took off at a quick pace, and at the two-mile mark, I was within range of my goal. Then, I bonked. My legs felt like lead. I had a hard time breathing. I staggered across the finish line, having missed my goal, though I did accomplish a personal best time. I was so exhausted afterwards that I had a hard time holding a water bottle and needed to sit down with my head between my knees so that I wouldn't fall over. Did I try my best? It would be easy to answer that I did, but in fact, I probably didn't. I could have trained a little harder or run the course ahead of time to better prepare. I could have run a

> **Alternatives to "Try Your Best"**
>
> - "Put in some great effort."
> - "Okay everyone, let's think really hard about this next challenge."
> - "Work at staying focused and engaged for the next 20 minutes."
> - "Let's brainstorm some ideas as a group. What would it look, sound, and feel like if we tried really hard during this work period?"

smarter race, saving a bit more for the end. If a tiger had suddenly appeared behind me in the last stretch of the race, I surely could have picked up the pace in the final tenth of a mile.

We've probably all told students to try their best. This may not be such helpful encouragement, though, because we can always look back at an effort and find a way it could have been better. For students who struggle with anxiety and put a lot of pressure on themselves, "Try your best" probably only adds to their feelings of stress. For students struggling with motivation, they may think, "There's no way I'm trying my best," and give up all together. For some other ideas of how to encourage hard work, consider ideas in the sidebar.

"*Just* Try Your Best."

Have you noticed how easy it is to let this little word (just) slide in? It's meant to soften—like what we're suggesting isn't such a big deal or shouldn't be that hard to do. We mean to ease anxiety and reassure students that everything's going to be okay: "It's okay, just try your best." When you really stop and think about it, what we're saying is that trying your best should be easy, which is actually the opposite of what we mean.

This word "just" may find its way into other unhelpful situations. "Just relax," we might say before a debate. "Just focus," we might say before a test. "Just pay attention," we might implore a class during a lesson. The message might be that relaxing, focusing, and paying attention are all easy to do—and that students already know how to do them. It's "just" a matter of doing it. Instead, we might offer more concrete suggestions. "As you work through this test, try spending your energy wisely—work at problems you know you can accomplish first." Or, "A debate can be intense. One way to relax is to close your eyes and take five deep cleansing breaths." Or, "Okay, everyone.

Turn your bodies toward me and listen carefully. This next set of directions will help you understand what to do next."

"It's Easy."

When we encourage students to try something or to invest their energy in something by saying, "It's easy" (or "Don't worry, it's easy!"), our intentions are once again good. We're trying to create the emotional space needed for students to take a risk. There are a couple of problems with this, though. First, by encouraging students to try something because it's easy, we are, in a sense, telling them that they shouldn't want to take on challenges. If easy stuff is good, hard stuff must be bad. Also, let's consider this from another perspective. Let's say you're a student who is nervous about being able to do something. You're hesitating with your work because you're worried you might fail. A teacher tries to reassure you: "Don't worry, it's easy!" Do you feel better? Perhaps you're encouraged by the tone of your teacher's voice, but might you even be more nervous about failing? What if it is easy and you still fail? Now you might really feel stupid!

Instead, if a student is feeling overwhelmed or nervous about starting something, we might encourage with more concrete advice: "Try the first problem, and see how it goes." Or we might help them find a starting point: "What's a question you have about this challenge?" Though it sounds counterintuitive, we might soften the emotional load by explaining the work as challenging: "Good luck with this challenge!" or "Let me know how I can support you when you need some help." By assuming that work is challenging and that help will be necessary, we might make it easier for students to take a risk and give things a shot.

Give More Formative Feedback

A quality of effective feedback—communication that leads to growth—is that it happens while the work is still in process. After all, when we give students feedback about their work after it's over, what are they supposed to do with that information? I remember making this mistake (many times) as a new teacher. At the end of a big project, I'd load students down with tons of information about what they did well and what could have been better. After independent research projects, I'd write up page-long narratives for students, packed with summative feedback. I was trying to help students learn from their work—understanding what qualities they should keep doing and which ones could be improved. The problem was that I was giving this information at the wrong time. Once the work was done, they couldn't do anything about it, and the next project was too far away to be remembered later with any kind of helpful clarity. Even as I worked at saving this feedback and having students review it as we began our next projects, the work was usually different enough that the feedback didn't always prove to be useful.

Instead, we should spend less time giving students summative feedback and shift toward giving them more formative feedback. We can confer with students as they work. We can jot encouragement and suggestions on sticky notes and attach them to rough drafts. We can have students submit in-process work with questions they have about elements of the assignment they're unsure of, giving us the chance to support and guide them individually before they get too far lost.

Giving students more formative feedback could also help with a common logistical problem in many secondary classrooms. In an effort to enable students to rework assignments to promote learning, many teachers allow students to redo tests, essays, and projects multiple times until students achieve the grade or assessment score they want. This can be a logistical nightmare for teachers as they end up assessing and grading assignments several times, sometimes weeks after units have finished. It can also create poor work habits in students as they learn that deadlines don't mean anything. They can turn in poor work and get to do it over and over again. If we give students more formative feedback, coaching, and support along the way, students can be successful by the time the actual deadline rolls around.

Offer Bite-Size, Within-Reach Pushes

According to John Hattie and Gregory Yates, students are "motivated by knowledge gaps, but put off by knowledge chasms" (2014, p. 6). This means that when we coach students, feedback must focus on doable, bite-size next steps. Giving students too much feedback or suggestions that are too challenging will overwhelm them to the point where they may give up. So, when conferring with a student in reading, you may notice several different strategies they could try. Choose one to focus on, and jot down the others so you can remember to check in on those another time. When reviewing a rough draft of a piece of writing, consider offering just a few key suggestions that will help the student revise. In the middle of an independent research project, you might see many possible ideas to offer students, but try to focus on just one or two suggestions at a time that will help keep their momentum moving forward.

I was observing a middle school band rehearsal and heard the teacher offer incredibly specific and bite-size feedback while also affirming students' progress and offering them a chance to think about improvements: "Yes! That's the right tempo—we're nailing that part. Now, let's look at line 33—it still sounds weak. What could we do to make it stronger?" Consider how powerful this feedback is while also being concise enough not to overwhelm or disrupt the flow of the rehearsal. Additionally, think about how good this bit of constructive criticism must have felt. By being honest with students about the weakness, this band teacher boosts students' sense of enthusiasm. It feels good when a coach gives constructive feedback that you can use to get better.

Focus Summative Feedback on Positives

I remember one of my teachers in middle school who seemed to relish the idea of making students feel bad after they turned in poor work. Her comments (written in red pen, of course) were scathing, and she used grades to humiliate. I once got a D with five minuses. I guess this was slightly better than my friend who got an $F+$. If her goal had been to turn her students off to learning, she couldn't have found a better mechanism. Hammering students with tons of negative feedback stifles motivation and shuts down learning. Unfortunately, the students who most need positive and supportive feedback (and whose sense of perseverance and self-confidences is lowest) are the ones who most receive overwhelming and negative feedback after work is complete. Let's keep in mind that the place for constructive feedback is while the work is in process. Once the work is finished, we should work at celebrating strengths to build enthusiasm and positive energy for upcoming work.

Encourage More Student Reflection

The most important feedback happens when we guide and support students in *their* learning as opposed to cajoling students—forcing them to do what we want them to do. Just as we explored in Chapter 9, we can boost student ownership of learning through encouraging student reflection. Let's now put this together with what we've been learning about encouraging a growth mindset. In the following examples, notice that growth is emphasized over intelligence and talent. Also notice that questions are open and inviting—they aren't about judging or comparing but are about thinking and learning (see Figure 12.4).

FIGURE 12.4

Before Work	During Work	After Work
• "What's a goal you have for this next piece of writing? Write that on a sticky note so I can ask you about it when we confer." • "Before we begin working on this next math challenge, think back to yesterday. What's a strategy that worked well for you as a mathematician? How might that help your learning today?" • "Turn and talk with a partner: What's a skill you're currently working on as a reader?"	• "Everyone, pause your work for a moment. Turn and talk with your lab partner—what's something that is going well for you right now in your science work? What's something that could be better?" • "Hi, Lisa. It's time to check in on your research project. Take a moment and look through your work. Decide on a spot where you'd like some support and coaching, and we'll begin there."	• "Look back over this latest piece of artwork. What's something that you're getting better at as an artist?" • "Look back through your math assessment. Circle three problems that you're proud of. Write a brief explanation about one of them." • "How do you think the concert went last night? What were some parts that were especially strong?"

Conclusion

Cherry McLaughlin was the principal of Flanders Elementary School in East Lyme, Connecticut during my first few formative years as a teacher. She was a wonderful leader in many ways. She encouraged faculty to take chances and make mistakes. She worked at sharing leadership with teachers, families, and students. She was joyful and energetic. One of the simplest things I remember—something that made a big impression on me as a young teacher—was the nameplate that she had on her office door. It didn't say "Principal" or "Dr. McLaughlin." Instead, it said, "Chief Learner." It was a simple and powerful message: We were a learning organization, and she was the lead learner. What if we all viewed ourselves as lead learners? What if we thought of school as a workshop where young apprentices came to learn the complex craft of learning and we were the master learners who helped pass along the skills and mindsets needed for all to become master learners?

13

Build a Positive Adult Community: Teachers Talk Together

The majority of this book is about the language we use with students, but we should also consider the language we use with each other. This has been made abundantly clear to me as I talk with teachers about language habits while working in schools. Once we've begun digging into language habits and patterns, a few predictable questions and dilemmas arise:

- "Are you going to work with administrators to help them with the language they use with staff? It's hard for us not to be sarcastic with students if we're being talked to that way!"
- "There's another adult who works in my room, and she isn't always respectful with me or my students. What should I do?"
- "Our grade level team has a hard time being direct with each other. We all feel like we're walking on eggshells when we try and discuss something."

Let's begin by remembering that just as we all have positive intentions when it comes to our students, we all have the best of intentions when it comes to working with each other. We all want to create positive, supportive, and vibrant adult learning communities. Not only does this make school a better place for teachers, it also creates the kind of schoolwide community where students can thrive. And, just as we sometimes engage in language with students that doesn't align with our intentions, the same goes for our work with each other. After all, we got into this profession because we're good at working with young people. But there's a shadow side to that—we're not always so good at working with adults!

There are a few reasons that the language we use with each other in schools is so important. First off, we are what we practice, so we need to make sure we're practicing language habits of respect, kindness, generosity of spirit, and empathy. The way we talk with each other about school and students shapes, reshapes, and reinforces our beliefs and behaviors. Staff room talk matters. Second, even when we're talking with each other and think we're out of earshot of our students, there's always a chance that a student (or parent or community member) might be nearby. When we are in a professional setting, we should speak professionally—always assuming that what we say may be heard (and repeated) by others. We are responsible for maintaining the professional integrity of our schools.

With all of that in mind, let's explore a few more language patterns that will help us build respectful and vibrant school communities. We'll begin by considering the language patterns that school leaders (administrators, curriculum coordinators, instructional coaches, department chairs, etc.) should consider when in a supervision and evaluation role. We'll then dig into language considerations for us all to think about in our daily interactions with colleagues.

School Leaders: Lead Great Learning with Faculty

Many of the language suggestions offered so far in this book translate directly to school leaders' work with faculty. If you're in a leadership role in your school or district, you are leading great learning with adult learners in the same way they should lead great learning with their students. This means that using supportive and positive language with staff serves two important goals. First, it helps create the conditions where teachers can thrive. You can encourage cooperation over competition, model a growth mindset, support positive adult identities, boost intrinsic motivation, and promote joyful learning communities. Second, you have an opportunity to model the kind of language habits that teachers can then use with students. Consider every faculty meeting, PLC meeting, grade-level meeting, and individual interaction with faculty as an opportunity to help teachers feel the effect of positive and supportive language practices and to give them examples of language they can use with their students.

Consider the sample strategies in Figure 13.1 that support adult learning communities where teachers feel energized and safe enough to take risks.

FIGURE 13.1	
Goals	**Strategies**
Create a culture of respect and collaboration.	• Reduce judgmental and comparative language. • Avoid manipulative praise.
Boost teachers' positive sense of self.	• Use preferred names and correct pronunciations. • Beware of implicit biases. • Reinforce teachers' high self-expectations.
Boost ownership and intrinsic motivation.	• Talk positively about school challenges. • Boost teacher interaction time during PD and faculty meetings. • Emphasize significance and purpose (instead of compliance) when discussing school goals.

These sample goals and strategies are just a few examples. I encourage you to come up with your own. Create your own chart with your goals on the left side and strategies that will support them on the right.

As I've worked with countless schools over the years, I have seen school leaders encounter a common challenge that you should know about. As teachers start to examine their own language practices, they may become hyper-aware of how school leaders are speaking to them. This can serve as fantastic motivation for leaders to work on their own language habits—both to create the kind of climate that supports great learning in the adult community and to model what it looks like to grow and learn as an educator. Leaders might even acknowledge to staff that they are working on a language goal and ask for teachers' understanding and support as they try and shift their own habits.

For teachers who are reading this, I'd like to encourage you to be kind and understanding with your school leaders as they work at shifting their own language. It can be easy to fall into the trap of saying, "I'm working at changing my language, but my principal keeps using sarcasm!" Remember that growth and learning take time, and you should allow your school leaders to be on the steep end of the learning curve. They'll need lots of practice. They'll need to make lots of mistakes. And, just like you, they shouldn't work on more than one language goal at a time.

Now let's consider language habits and patterns that we all might bear in mind—whether or not we're in a leadership role—that will help create the kinds of school communities where all members are safe, are valued, and can flourish as learners.

Try Not to Judge Students and Families

Of course, we all want to demonstrate respect for our students and their families. This is easy when we're feeling calm and successful—not quite so simple when we're upset or feeling incompetent. After a rough day, where multiple lessons fall flat and students are unruly, it is harder to have empathy for students who are struggling. By early December, as we hit the predictable energy slump before the winter break, we may find it hard not to lapse into grumping and grousing in the staff room. When we see families with seemingly very different priorities and values from our own, we might be too quick to judge negatively, which can easily lead to gossiping. So, let's keep a couple of important ideas in mind. Just as all kids want to be successful (even though they may show the reverse as a defense mechanism), all parents and families want what's best for their children, even when they seem to behave in ways that show the opposite. For example, the same student who doesn't have enough money to buy properly fitting clothes, afford school lunch, or bring in money for a field trip might also always have the newest smartphone and brag about his gaming system at home. It's so easy for us to make a snap judgment: His parents just don't care about school. In fact, what we're probably seeing is simply a different value system at work.

Even judgments that feel positive can be problematic. A personal pet peeve of mine is when adults say, "Oh! They're such *good* kids!" Though this is meant to show love and kindness, there may be hidden messages here. Does this mean that other kids aren't *good* kids? I'd hope we wouldn't describe some kids as bad, but *good* is a relative term, isn't it? We've probably all seen *good* kids excused from poor choices because of their positive reputation. For example, teachers might hear rumors about the soccer team drinking in the woods after a game and turn a blind eye ("After all, those kids get good grades and come from good families—they're good kids").

For a couple of ideas about how to shift away from judgment when talking about students and families, check out Figure 13.2.

FIGURE 13.2

Instead of ...	Move from ...	Try This ...
"Vicki's parents just don't care about school. They can't even get her here on time!"	Negative to positive assumption	"Vicki's parents are probably really overwhelmed. It's hard for them to get her here on time."
"You're coaching the swim team? Oh, they're such good kids!"	Judging to describing	"You're coaching the swim team? I've had several swimmers in my classes and they've been responsible and kind."

Avoid Labeling Students

Just as we shouldn't address students with labels, we should resist using them when talking about students with colleagues. Slapping labels on students has become so commonplace in schools that we probably don't even realize we're doing it. Students who attend the vocational program at the high school are called "voc kids." Students who receive special education supports are "SPED kids." Students who are learning English are "ELLs." Students with high IQs are labeled "gifted." At the high school that my son and daughter attend, students from a nearby town, Barrington, can pay tuition to attend. They're commonly referred to by students, teachers, and administration as "the Barrington kids"—a label that (unintentionally) carries some undertones of classism. I've even heard of some schools who refer to their students on the edge of proficient in standardized tests as "bubble kids."

This kind of labeling puts students into narrow boxes and tends to frame students' identities around one trait—as if learning English, having a high raw intelligence, or being from Barrington is their defining quality. Students are multifaceted and come to us with a variety of strengths, challenges, and characteristics. Another danger of this sort of labeling is that it tends to group students together by a given characteristic, which may narrow how we see students.

That being said, there are times we need to talk about students who share a common characteristic. Or, we may need to talk about a specific characteristic of a child because it's important to the context of the conversation. If that's the case, we should use what is called people-first language: Name the child first and the characteristic second. Consider the examples in Figure 13.3:

FIGURE 13.3	
Instead of . . .	**Try This . . .**
"We're here to discuss how to best support homeless families."	"We're here to discuss how to support families experiencing homelessness."
"All band kids please report to the auditorium for a group picture."	"All students who are members of the band, please report to the auditorium for a group picture."
"Jimmy is a Down's kid."	"Jimmy has Down syndrome."
"I've got three ADHD kids in my second period class this year."	"There are three students in my second period class who have ADHD."

Finally, I think it's worth reconsidering common cutesy names we have for students that we may use with each other as we talk about them. I've heard many 1st grade teachers refer to their students as "firsties" when discussing their class. Many of us may use "kiddos" as we discuss our students. Just as we explored in Chapter 3, we should be cautious about referring to students in ways that can feel belittling. Even when we're talking to each other and students aren't around, there's a level of mental rehearsal involved in this kind of language that warrants caution.

Speak Professionally About Students

A colleague of mine was in a meeting, and a substitute teacher was in his class. I walked by his room and was stunned by what I saw. His normally in-control 3rd graders were behaving horribly. They were jumping out of their seats and running around the room. They were calling out and yelling. They were giving the substitute wrong information about the rules and routines of the room. Chaos reigned. I stepped in and helped settle the room, but I was fuming mad. Later I saw my colleague. "Your kids were being a bunch of jerks!" I spouted as I recounted all that I had seen. He was, of course, upset, and he went back to his class and let them have it—including mentioning that I had said they were acting like a bunch of jerks. A few days later, due to an irate parent who had called our principal, we were both making a public apology to his class. (I had actually used a much worse word than "jerks," and he softened my language as he spoke to his class—thank heaven.) Regardless, it was a bad call for me to use a derogatory term about his students. It only inflamed the situation, and there were other ways that what I said could have come to light. Another staff member could have heard what I said and shared it with a parent. A parent could have been walking by. When we're in school, we should use language we would be comfortable with others repeating.

Additionally, as we'll dig into further in the next chapter, we become what we rehearse. As we talk with colleagues about our students, I think we should be aware that we're engaging in a form of practice. So, ask yourself, are you talking about your students in ways you want to feel about them?

Stop Using the Language of War

Here's another way we may accidentally rehearse and practice emotions that we don't want to nurture. Have you noticed how words associated with warfare creep into the way we speak about school? When we refer to our ourselves as being "in the trenches" or we say we're "on the front lines," what are we implying about our schools and how we feel about them? We might talk about "rallying the troops" as we call students in from recess or say that we're going to "bite the bullet" and have a tough phone call with a parent. I once heard a teacher say that "we need more boots on the ground" when talking about the need for more lunchroom monitors.

Let's be honest, some days are hard. Some schools, where gang violence means that staff can't walk safely to their cars at dusk, might feel like a war zone. But let's be careful about what we reinforce. If we constantly feed into the narrative that we're at war—that our students are either fellow combatants or enemy troops—how will we ever create schools that feel safe and joyful?

Handling Differences and Conflict

Just as we could never expect to have a class of students work together for a whole year without any conflict arising, we should understand that the same is true for our adult communities. During a staff meeting, someone will throw out an idea and have it shot down by a colleague in a less than supportive way. In a department or grade-level team, there will be disagreements about common assessments. Strong personalities will clash during a professional development workshop. This is just part of the deal when working with other people. It's how we handle these kinds of challenges that can make or break an adult learning community.

The first thing to do, if someone has said or done something that you found upsetting, is to decide if the issue needs to be addressed. If you can take a deep breath and move on, you might let it go. Let's not create unnecessary drama that will take our energy away from our students!

Some issues, however, do need to be addressed. Perhaps your feelings have been hurt and you need to deal with it to move on. Or, you're worried that similar interactions might happen again if it's not dealt with. Here are a few tips for navigating conflict with colleagues:

- **Cool off first.** Before addressing a challenge with a colleague, give yourself some time to get in control. Confronting someone when overly upset or angry is a surefire way to do or say something you'll regret later. You may also bring energy to the conversation that will escalate instead of deescalate a situation.
- **Be direct.** When you need to let people know that they have upset you, the best course of action is usually to just tell them—clearly and directly. Don't talk about them behind closed doors. Don't drop hints or retaliate subtly. (Many teachers have told me that passive-aggressiveness is common and destructive in their school's adult community.) Once you're calm, let your colleague know that you need to talk something through: "I was upset by something that happened between us yesterday when we were up in front of parents during our open house talk, and I need to let you know about it."
- **Use "I statements."** Speaking in the first person can help someone hearing that they upset you feel more empathy and understanding. Speaking in the second person—"You made me mad when . . ."— tends to put people on the defensive, which can make it hard to have a productive conversation. For example, instead of beginning with, "You said something yesterday that really upset me," you might say, "I was really upset by something you said yesterday."
- **Assume best intentions.** Have you noticed that when someone else upsets you, it can be easy to assume that they were being thoughtless or intentionally disrespectful, but when we are the ones who make the mistake, we expect others to give us the benefit of the doubt? (I was driving in Los Angeles and was cut off by another driver. "Jerk," I muttered. Not five minutes later, trying to sneak through

an intersection before a light turned red, I cut off someone else. "I'm from out of town, sorry," I said to myself.) Perhaps we should always begin by assuming that when others do something we find upsetting or offensive, they were having a bad day or were tired or had other things on their mind. With this in mind, you might begin a tough conversation by saying, "I'm sure you didn't mean to hurt my feelings the other day during our PLC meetings, but I wanted to let you know why I was upset."

We should also acknowledge that this is *hard*. "Have you tried talking it out?" rolls off our tongues so easily when a student looks for help in solving a conflict with a peer. Then it comes time for us to confront a colleague, and we discover it's not so easy. Still, it's almost always worth it. When we can engage in healthy conflict in a school—when grievances can be aired with professionalism and kindness—and when adults can learn to iron out difficulties with each other, our schools can finally start to really move forward.

What If an Adult I Work with Speaks with Students Unprofessionally?

A specific kind of conflict may arise between adults who work together with students as we begin to work on language. After all, when more than one adult works in a room, it's likely that they will have different language habits and patterns. This is normal and isn't in and of itself a bad thing. Even though we may work toward more consistent language practices in a school, we should never try to be so consistent that we lose our individual voices. It's okay for students to learn that different teachers have different temperaments—some may be serious and others silly, some energetic and others more relaxed.

Still, there are some kinds of language that aren't appropriate or professional, and if you work with an adult who uses these kinds of language habits with students, you may need to address this challenge.

Here's an example from my own experience as a classroom teacher. One year I had an adult in my classroom who was there to support a student who had some profound special needs. In many ways, she was a wonderful addition to our 5th grade classroom. She was a free spirit and was kind and generous. Students enjoyed her sense of humor, and she was always ready to help anyone who needed it. And—and this was a big "and"—every now and then, she would let an inappropriate comment fly with students. I'll never forget the day that two boys were chatting with her before our morning meeting. They found out that it was her birthday, and they said, "Happy birthday! What do you want for your birthday?" Her response, "Johnny Depp covered in chocolate," was clearly not appropriate for 5th graders.

Here was an opportunity for me to practice some of the advice offered in the last section. First, I gave myself time to think—not responding in the moment when I was upset. Later, I was clear and direct while also assuming best intentions. "Cathy, I know you weren't meaning to be inappropriate earlier with Cory and Pedro, but the Johnny Depp comment wasn't okay." Fortunately, she agreed immediately and apologized. What if she hadn't? What if she had defended her comment and had said it wasn't a big deal? I would have been more direct: "Even if you don't agree, it wasn't okay with me. It doesn't fit with the culture I'm trying to create with these students."

These conversations can be hard. They're also necessary. If we hear a colleague cracking jokes that are off-color or derogatory, if we hear a colleague using sarcasm or threatening language, or if we hear other language that doesn't fit with the culture and climate that students need to thrive in schools, we must say something. Silence signals acceptance. If we can't confront that colleague directly, we might ask a colleague or administrator for support or guidance. What's important is that we do something. We are all responsible for creating kind, nurturing, and supportive school environments for our students.

Conclusion

As I was writing this book, I talked with many teachers about it, and I was surprised at the number who asked some version of, "Are you going to have something in there about how adults talk with each other in schools?" When I said that I was, most responded with relief. It's pretty clear that many of us need some work in this area! Perhaps the one key idea to keep in mind is to apply the same level of professionalism, respect, empathy, and joyfulness that we want to use with our students to the interactions we have with each other.

14

Shift Your Language Patterns

Habits and routines are important. They help us get through each day. You probably make coffee or cook breakfast in a similar fashion every morning. You likely commute to and from work the same way every day. When you shop for groceries, don't you tend to follow a similar routine each time— snaking your way through the aisles in a predictable pattern and getting the same brands of milk, dishwashing liquid, and cereal? If you think about it, you might be surprised at how much of your daily life is habitual. You tend to run on autopilot.

This is a good thing. Habits enable us to keep our minds available to think about things that aren't routine (Schneider & Shiffrin, 1977). You can plan your daughter's birthday party while you take a shower because you don't have to think about how to shower. Our language habits in school are no different. There is no way we could function if we had to analyze everything we said before we said it. Just imagine: "Okay. I'm about to have my students line up to head outside. What should I call them? Do I ask a question or make a statement? What should my tone sound like?" By the time we got through all of this processing, the kids would already be outside, leaving us still pondering in the doorway. We have to rely on language habits and patterns.

And because habits are, well, habitual, they can be really hard to change. This is especially true when the habits we're in yield short-term benefits, even if they don't pay off in the long run—and even when we have the best of intentions (Jager, 2003; Ouellette & Wood, 1998). We know that eating cookies in the afternoon yields a long-term negative outcome (poorer health). However, if we're in a habit of eating cookies each afternoon, the immediate pleasure of eating the cookies makes it hard not to do so. If we're in the habit of using sarcasm (which can feel pleasurable in the moment), it can be hard to stop, even though we know it doesn't fit with our long-term goal of creating a safe and supportive learning environment. Whether we're trying to adopt a new exercise routine, shift the way we eat, or change the way we give students positive feedback, shifting habits requires conscious effort and hard work. That's the bad news—it ain't easy.

But, take heart, there's also some good news. Once the new habit has been formed, it no longer requires much effort to stay there. We've now created the new autopilot setting. That's what this chapter is all about: practical strategies for reprogramming our autopilot.

Before we dive into the process and some strategies for shifting language patterns, I think it's first important to address a potential emotional barrier. It can be hard to acknowledge that we need to make a change because that means that we have been making a mistake (perhaps for years!). This can be hard to swallow. Teaching, like few other professions, is not just a job for most of us—it is a calling. Being a teacher is central to our core identify. We don't just teach—we *are teachers*. If we've been making a mistake, especially with something as fundamental as the way we talk with students, this can feel like a huge failure. Shame and guilt might begin to surface, and when they do, we quickly jump to our own defense. "But I mean well," we might reason. "Kids understand when I use sarcasm. They know I'm joking," we explain. "Kids don't think I'm talking down to them," we rationalize. "I'm a good teacher." And there it is. Because we *are teachers*, if we start to feel as though we've been making a mistake that might have not been good for our students, this can be a serious blow to our egos. Once we're in this emotional state, it can be awfully hard to break out and make a shift. When our defenses are up, we block ourselves from learning.

It might be helpful to consider a quote that hangs on the wall of the conference room at Fairgrounds Elementary School in Nashua, New Hampshire: "What we learn today doesn't make us bad yesterday, it makes us better tomorrow." We all have language habits that need refining, and beating ourselves up about it isn't going to do anyone any good. As I'm writing this sentence, there are a few of my own that immediately surface in my own mind. Just the other day, my son said, "Dad. I can't always tell when you're serious and when you're joking," the exact same feedback that Jenna gave me almost 25 years ago. *I still have plenty of room to grow.* Perhaps we should all practice not being so hard on ourselves—what Tom Newkirk names self-generosity—the "capacity to keep going in the face of difficulty" (2017, p. 188).

The rest of this chapter is intended to give you a clear pathway for making important shifts in your language once you give yourself permission to grow. The first section will outline a three-step process that will lead to change that sticks. Then, we'll move into a bunch of concrete and practical strategies to make the shifts you want.

A Three-Step Process for Changing Language

Changing a language habit, like changing any other habit, requires thoughtful attention, planning, practical strategies, and feedback.

Step 1: Set a Good Goal and Have a Meaningful Rationale

This first step begins with two important questions to ask yourself. What is the language habit that I want to shift, and why is this so important? The first question is about identifying a goal. Are you looking to change the way you give positive feedback? Do you want to work on changing the way you name a class? Do you want to reduce your use of sarcasm or move up the hierarchy of moral reasoning when talking with students about discipline?

Good goals are bite-size and manageable. Instead of taking on an overwhelming goal such as, "I want to change the way I give feedback," you might consider a small goal within that broader challenge. Perhaps you want to reduce the number of times you begin positive feedback with "I like," or perhaps you want to move from general praise ("Great job!") to more specific feedback ("You used three different problem-solving strategies during that math challenge!").

It's also important to recognize that one goal is plenty to tackle at any given time. In my experience, taking on more than one language change goal is overwhelming.

Before you take this goal and run with it, however, you also need to answer the second question: Why is this so important? Shifting your language is hard work. It's will take time. You're going to get frustrated. What is it about this goal that makes it worth your time and energy? If you can't answer this second question with a rationale that is personally emotionally compelling, you'll likely have a hard time sticking with the work as it gets hard.

When I worked at shifting away from the habit of beginning positive feedback with phrases such as "I like the way you . . ." and "I love it when . . .", I had a clear and compelling rationale: I wanted my students to become more independent and to be less reliant on me. The more I hooked them in with teacher-pleasing language, the more dependent on me they became. Because this goal had a lot of personal meaning for me, it gave me the motivation I needed to put in the hard work that was necessary.

I remember a time when I picked a goal with a rationale that didn't hold as much meaning. My wife and I taught in the same school for several years, and at one point she noticed a language habit that she thought I should consider. "Have you noticed that you call all of your students, both boys and girls, 'guys?'" Heather asked. I'd never really thought about it before. She pushed, "Wouldn't it be weird if you started calling all of your students 'girls?'" She had a point. I would walk up to a group of two boys and two girls and say, "Okay, guys, it's time to start cleaning up." Or, I'd sit down with two girls who were playing a math game and say, "How's it going, guys?" I felt a little embarrassed. I consider myself thoughtful about gender issues and would never want girls in my class to think that I was being disrespectful. Right away, I decided to change how I addressed girls and mixed-gender groups. I started using "girls" for groups of girls, though this felt weird because now I felt like I was focusing on gender when addressing students. For mixed-gender groups I used terms like "5th graders" and "everyone," which felt fine. After a while though, I lost steam. I slipped back into my old habit.

There were a few reasons this one didn't stick, I think. First, I realized that the term "guys" actually felt fairly gender-neutral. Girls in my class addressed each other this way. I even heard female colleagues address friends in the staffroom with, "Hey, guys!" More importantly though, I realized that I failed to make a compelling case for myself. The impetus for the change came from Heather, and although I understood her point of view, I didn't take the time needed to make it my point of view as well. It wasn't until years later, when I did more reflecting on gender bias, that I made this shift successfully.

As you consider changes you might make, spend some time articulating *why* this shift is important. Don't change because a colleague wants you to. For goodness sake, don't change because some knucklehead who wrote a book thinks it's a good idea. Change because it will help your students feel safer or be more engaged learners or grow into responsible and

A Few Sample Good Goals

- Replace, "I like the way you . . ." and "Good job!" with more specific nonjudgmental feedback to help students know what they're doing well and to boost intrinsic motivation.

- Shift from first person to second person when discussing work and learning to help students feel more ownership of work.

- Use more open-ended questions (and fewer closed ones) during academic discussions to facilitate richer conversations.

- When discussing behavior, move up the moral hierarchy to explain the "why," to help students learn to think about how their behaviors can positively impact others.

- Talk about learning and work in positive and joyful ways to boost enthusiasm for learning.

caring adults. Change because you want your language to better align with your positive beliefs and best goals for your students.

Step 2: Plan Concrete Strategies for Action and Feedback

Once you've got a goal and compelling rationale, choose one or two strategies you might use to help you break your old habit and set up the new one. Look for strategies that will provide you with concrete guidance on what to do differently. Also look for strategies that will give you meaningful feedback. Many of the following section's strategies do both.

The strategy you choose should feel doable, not overwhelming. It should feel relevant. It should also be fun, if possible. My friend and colleague, Tom Newkirk, and I were talking once about the importance of the role of pleasure in daily exercise routines. He made the point that if you're ever going to stick with an exercise plan, you have to find a way of exercising that's enjoyable. Even with the best of goals and intentions for staying healthy, if you don't like the daily exercise you've chosen, it will be hard to maintain momentum. Tom loves to swim, so going to the pool five times a week is enjoyable—and even on the days when he might be inclined to skip a practice, he can get himself to the pool because he knows he'll like it once he gets in. On the other hand, he hates to run, so if he were to try and run to stay in shape, he'd have a much harder time getting himself out there. As you explore this chapter's strategies, think of ones that will make the practice and work itself enjoyable.

Finally, because habits help reduce our cognitive load—enabling us to do one thing while thinking about another—you might consider focusing your language practice during a time of the day when you feel particularly comfortable, when another part of your teaching can run on autopilot (at least a little bit). For example, if you have a solid routine set up for writing workshop—your students are independent and you have predictable routines (such as conferring with students and pulling small groups of students for strategy work) that you've practiced, this might be an especially good time to focus your energy on shifting a language habit.

Step 3: Practice and Consolidate

Once you've articulated a goal and rationale and you've chosen some concrete strategies to try, you're ready for the most challenging step. It's time to put in the hard work needed to make the change stick. You should expect that this will take a long time. Consider two different phases of this final stage. The first is about practice, practice, practice. Learning a new serve in tennis, a new flip turn in swimming, or a new knitting technique involves tons of practice. The goal is muscle memory—practicing the new skill enough so that it becomes automatic.

You've made your language charts and hung them around the room. Now use them. You've created a recording of the language you want to use. Listen to it over and over. You've got a colleague coming in to listen for the number of times you say some version of "I expect you all to . . ." (instead of "Next you get to . . ."). When is she coming in again?

I remember a veteran colleague of mine once giving me a calculation for how long it takes to shift into a new habit: one week for every year you've been alive. That seems high to me—perhaps she was trying to scare me into getting into good habits at the beginning of my career. Her point is a good one, though: The longer you've been in a habit, the harder it is to undo. I know that shifting away from "I like the way you . . ." took me a *long* time. It was probably most of a school year for the language to begin to feel normal and even longer for it to be truly automatic.

And this brings up the second part to this phase. First, we have to put in the repetition needed to begin to form a new habit. Then, there's a transition phase, where we begin to see the new habit forming and we're likely to say, "Yes! I've got it!" and move onto the next challenge. There's a danger here, though. We have to remain vigilant. It's so easy to slip back into old habits if we don't keep paying attention. So, keep practicing, keep checking in, and keep noticing your language habit as it solidifies. Focus on consolidation so that your new habit truly becomes automatic—the new autopilot.

Now, let's consider some practical strategies you can use to help you practice!

Practical Strategies for Changing Language Habits

The following strategies are ones that I have found helpful, either when working on a language habit of my own or while helping other teachers shift their language patterns. This is by no means an exhaustive list. In addition to these ideas, consider other fun ways you might work on your language—ones that will work well for you.

Create a T-Chart

Throughout this book, I've tried to include lots of charts to suggest some language changes you might consider. The goal of these charts is to offer replacements for language habits you might have. It's like how Weight Watcher participants are encouraged to find replacements for unhealthy foods. You like having a salty and crunchy snack in the afternoon? Try popcorn instead of potato chips. You like to sip cold carbonated drinks throughout the day? Drink a seltzer instead of a sugary soda.

These charts are only meant to be starting points. The specific words given in the charts may or may not work for you, for we each have our own unique voice (vocabulary, idioms, slang we use). Make your own T-chart. Put your goal at the top of the chart and then label the columns "Instead of..." and "Try This...." In the "Instead of" column, jot down some of the things you say that you're trying to change. In the "Try This" column, write down what you'll say instead. Include examples that sound and feel as natural as possible (understanding that any new habit will feel unnatural at first). Use charts in this book for inspiration, but make sure to craft examples that will work for you.

Next, find a place to keep this chart where you can refer to it easily. You might place a smaller copy in a few places you commonly look throughout the day. You might even copy and paste it right onto the plans for lessons that you use.

Post Reminders in Your Room

Another way to give yourself concrete reminders of the language you're trying to use is to place larger visual aids around your room. This was a strategy that really helped me as I was working at moving away from "I like." I made posters that read "I notice . . .", "Tell me more about . . .", and "What do you think about. . . ." I also created one that said "*Pause!*" to remind myself that I didn't always have to say something. I posted these suggestions around the perimeter of my room, at the top of my walls near the ceiling. This meant that I could see them wherever I was and they wouldn't distract from anchor charts that the students used throughout the day. Then, when a student came up to me with a piece of work saying, "Mr. Anderson, here's a poem I just wrote!" and I could feel an "I like the way you . . ." coming, I could glance up at my walls and use a different sentence starter. "Wow! I notice that you used alliteration in the first couple of lines. That can make a poem come alive for a reader!"

Of course, my students noticed the posters and wanted to know what they were for, which brings us to another strategy.

Share Your Goal with Your Students

If you really want to commit to changing a language habit, there might not be a better strategy than telling your students about it. First, once you tell your students, you're really committed. Good luck backing out now! Second, you can ask your students to support you as you work toward your new goal. You might say, "One of the ways I'm growing as a teacher right now is by shifting a language habit I have. I have realized that I sometimes talk about schoolwork as if I own it and you're all working for me. For example, I might say, 'Here's what you're going to do for me.' I want to try and stop saying 'for me' so much. When you hear me say that, would you be willing to give me a gentle reminder?" In my experience, students are usually more than willing to help!

Before we move on to another strategy, let's just consider a potential side-benefit of using this strategy. We get to model authentic professional growth and learning. We're likely going to model struggling, having to work hard to meet a goal, and how to handle frustration. Could there be a better way to demonstrate what real learning looks like than to be learners ourselves in front of our students?

Observe Yourself

One of the great challenges of shifting language habits is that most of our habits are unconscious. That can make them awfully hard to work on. Plus, when we need to work on them, we're also doing something else—namely teaching, which involves an incredibly complex skill set, requiring attention, focus, concentration, and shifting and adjusting on the fly. How are we supposed to listen to (and adjust!) our language in the midst of teaching when our cognitive load is high?

One strategy that can really help is to record yourself as you teach. Try using a smartphone or tablet to record a lesson, a writing conference, or whatever you want to listen to. You might use video, especially if you're interested in examining your body language—posture, facial expressions, gestures, and so on. Or, you might use the voice memo setting to just record sound. Just knowing that you're recording yourself will likely raise your awareness of language in the moment. In addition to helping you practice in the moment, this is also a great way to track your progress. You might try recording yourself once a week during a similar block of time for a month to see if you're habit is shifting.

Try Collegial Coaching

Is there a more powerful (or untapped) form of professional development than collegial coaching? I suppose this is a debatable point, but I haven't yet found one. When we get into each other's classrooms and support each other through authentic supportive feedback, our practice can really take off. It is beyond the scope of this book to fully explain effective collegial coaching, so I'll offer just a few tips so that if you'd like to have a colleague support your language, you have a starting place.

- **Have one or two clear goals.** Share these goals so that your classroom observer knows what to watch and listen for. Avoid having colleagues come in to observe and just give feedback about whatever they notice. This is too open for the observer and can lead to unhelpful feedback.

- **Ask for feedback in a roughly 3:1 ratio.** Consider asking for three positives and a push or six positives and two pushes. It's important that we know what we're doing well and have some ideas to grow on. The 3:1 ratio keeps the emphasis on positive feedback while also giving us the pushes we want to improve our practice.
- **Keep observation and feedback sessions short.** Too much feedback, even when it's positive and constructive, is overwhelming. There's just so much we can take in at once. Also, we rarely have enough time in our schedules to observe in each other's rooms for an hour at a time. Although we all have the best of intentions, I've seen many schools offer the idea of creating observation schedules where administrators will provide coverage, and few actually follow through. Try touching base briefly before the observation to be clear about goals, have a short observation time (10–15 minutes is a good starting place), and then debrief later for 3–5 minutes, perhaps during lunch or right after school.
- **Maintain positive relationships.** Ask trusted colleagues to observe you and offer you feedback. It can feel risky to have others observe you in action, especially when you're working on something challenging. You'll be better able to receive constructive feedback from someone you trust.

Practice in Other Settings

Part of learning any new skill is putting in the time and repetition needed to develop automaticity. We've got to practice, practice, practice. When I was moving away from the teacher-pleasing language of "I like the way you . . ." and toward more observational feedback, I practiced with my cat. "Peter, I see that you brought a bird to the door." "You jumped up on the couch, Peter!" A bit goofy, perhaps, but it helped!

You might use your commute to practice. Have a phrase or two that you want to work on and use your time in the car to practice saying the phrases, with the tone and expression you're going for, over and over. Once I was driving from New Hampshire to Virginia where, among other things, I was going to record a video interview about a book I had written. I had been given the questions ahead of time, so I wrote my responses and used the voice memo app on my phone to record myself reading them aloud. Several times on my trip, I listened to myself answering the interview questions as a way of practicing, and it was amazing how comfortable and prepared I felt when I got on camera. You could try this with language you're working on: Record yourself using the language (pay attention to tone!) you want to use and listen to yourself over and over.

Notice that this is another strategy that helps lighten the cognitive load required to learn a new skill. By practicing language when you have more time to think, you can focus more of your energy on the language habit you're trying to develop. This can allow the new pattern to become more automatic so that it can be used during more complex times later (like while teaching a new activity to a group of students).

Fake It 'Til You Become It

It might be that you have read something in this book that struck a nerve, but you're feeling anxious about it. What if you read about an idea and are thinking about a shift, but when you're really honest with yourself, you're not quite buying it yet? It might be that you really want to want students to feel more ownership for their work, but you're not sure you do yet. Or, maybe you wish that you wanted students to feel independent and strong, but there's a part of you that really loves it when they rely on you for their sense of self—it feels so good when they look to you for approval.

Part of what can be so hard about changing language patterns is that the new language feels unnatural at first. "I just don't sound like me," we might think. There might even be a little embarrassment or nervousness about the change. I remember feeling self-conscious when I started wearing a tie as a teacher. My first few years in the classroom, I tended to dress pretty casually—short-sleeved shirts and khakis were the norm. Jeans weren't unusual. In warm weather, I often donned shorts and sandals. When I decided to shift my attire to a more professional style—nice pants, button-down shirts, and ties—it felt weird. But not for long. It was only a matter of a few weeks before the new norm felt, well, normal.

We've probably all heard about the idea of faking it until we make it. If we just pretend long enough, eventually we'll make the change. As it turns out, there's a whole raft of research that supports the idea that this is exactly what happens. Here's an interesting one: Participants in one study were asked to work on multitasking activities designed to induce stress. They were trained to hold chopsticks in their mouths in one of three ways (neutral, standard smile, genuine smile that involved eye muscles). Participants who had standard and genuine smiles had lower heart rates after recovery from the activities (Kraft & Pressman, 2012). In another study, participants in a speed-dating setting who pretended to already be in love with the people they were meeting (they touched their hands as they talked, gazed lovingly into each other's eyes, and whispered) more than doubled their interest in seeing prospective dates again (Alleyne, 2012). In short, pretending to be in love appeared to boost actual romantic interest!

Amy Cuddy is a social psychologist who has done extensive research into the science of body language. In a fascinating TED Talk (2012), she explains that our own body language can change the way we feel about ourselves. Adopting a powerful pose for two minutes, standing tall with shoulders back and arms extended for example, can boost testosterone levels and decrease cortisol (a stress hormone) levels. Conversely, adopting a submissive pose for two minutes, sitting hunched forward with arms in and head down for example, decreases testosterone levels while raising cortisol levels. What we do changes how we feel. Cuddy finishes her TED talk with a powerful message about changing our self-perceptions. She encourages us, when working at personal change, to not just fake it 'til we make it, but to work at true internalization: to fake it 'til we become it.

This is, perhaps, one of the most hopeful aspects of this exploration of shifting language habits. As we work toward making our language better match our best intentions and positive goals for our students, we may in fact help ourselves get closer to becoming the teachers we want to be.

Conclusion

There is so much in education right now that is challenging. Many children come to school lacking skills of school readiness or having experienced trauma at home. Districts purchase stale boxed curricula in an attempt to meet the unrealistic demands of standardized tests that fail to measure what we know is most important. Funding for schools continues to be low, and many teachers don't earn enough to support a family. This can all feel so dispiriting, and it can make real change feel out of reach—something we can't control.

Changing our teacher language can't fix any of this. However, our language is something *we can control*. It doesn't require school board approval or a districtwide initiative to begin. It's not subject or grade level dependent but instead is an integral part of every subject and for every age. The way we talk about learning, behavior, and every other aspect of school has a profound effect on how students feel and how ready they are to learn. So, let's continue to work at creating learning environments where all children can learn, grow, and thrive!

References

Alleyne, R. (2012, July 4). Watch out lotharios: Faking romantic feelings can actually lead to the real thing. *The Telegraph.* Retrieved from http://www.telegraph.co.uk/news/science/science-news/9373087/Watch-out-lotharios-Faking-romantic-feelings-can-actually-lead-to-the-real-thing.html

Amemiya, J., & Wang, M. (2018). Why effort praise can backfire in adolescents. Retrieved from https://onlinelibrary.wiley.com/doi/abs/10.1111/cdep.12284

Blatt, M., & Kohlberg, L. (1975). The effects of classroom moral discussion upon children's level of moral judgment. *Journal of Moral Education, 4*(2), 129–161.

Brown, D. (2002). *Becoming a successful urban teacher.* Portsmouth, NH: Heinemann.

Charney, R. (2002). *Teaching children to care: Management in the responsive classroom.* Turners Falls, MA: Northeast Foundation for Children.

Costa, A. L., & Kallick, B. (Eds.). (2008). *Learning and leading with habits of mind: 16 essential characteristics for success.* Alexandria, VA: ASCD.

Crowe, C. (2012). *How to bullyproof your classroom.* Turners Falls, MA: Northeast Foundation for Children.

Cuddy, A. (2012, June). Your body language may shape who you are [Video file]. Retrieved from https://www.ted.com/talks/amy_cuddy_your_body_language_shapes_who_you_are

Deci, E. (1995). *Why we do what we do: Understanding self-motivation.* New York: Penguin Group.

Deci, E., Koestner, R., & Ryan, R. (1999). A meta-analytic review of experiments examining the effects of extrinsic rewards on intrinsic motivation. *Psychological Bulletin, 125*(6), 627–668.

Denton, P. (2007). *The power of our words: Teacher language that helps children learn.* Turners Falls, MA: Northeast Foundation for Children.

Dousis, A. (2007, April 1). What teaching Matthew taught me. *Responsive Classroom Newsletter.* https://www.responsiveclassroom.org/what-teaching-matthew-taught-me/

Duckworth, A. (2016). *Grit: The power of passion and perseverance.* New York: Scribner.

Dweck, C. (2006). *Mindset: The new psychology of success.* New York: Ballantine Books.

Dweck, C. (2016, January 11). Recognizing and overcoming false growth mindset [blog post]. *Edutopia.* Retrieved from https://www.edutopia.org/blog/recognizing-overcoming-false-growth-mindset-carol-dweck

Englander, E., & Schank, K. (2010, October 6). Reducing bullying and cyberbullying: Ten easy tips for educators can help prevent bullying in schools and online. Retrieved from https://www.eschoolnews.com/2010/10/06/reducing-bullying-and-cyberbullying/

Fendick, F. (1990). *The correlation between teacher clarity of communication and student achievement gain: A meta-analysis.* Unpublished doctorate, University of Florida.

Fiarman, S. (2016). Unconscious bias: When good intentions aren't enough. *Educational Leadership, 74*(3), 10–15.

Frizzell, M., Braun, M., Ferguson, M., Rentner, D. S., & Kober, N. (2017, May 31). *Building competencies for careers: Linking O*NET's occupational elements with deeper learning competencies.* Washington, DC: Center on Education Policy.

Gardner, H. (2011). *Frames of mind: The theory of multiple intelligences.* New York: Basic Books.

Greene, R. W. (2005). *The explosive child: A new approach for understanding and parenting easily frustrated, chronically inflexible children.* New York: HarperCollins.

Halsey, V. (2011). *Brilliance by design: Creating learning experiences that connect, inspire, and engage.* San Francisco, CA: Berrett-Koehler Publishers.

Hattie, J. (2009). *Visible learning: A synthesis of over 800 meta-analyses relating to achievement.* Abingdon, OX: Routledge.

Hattie, J., & Yates, G. (2014). *Visible learning and the science of how we learn.* New York: Routledge.

Himmele, P., & Himmele, W. (2017). *Total participation techniques: Making every student an active learner* (2nd ed.). Alexandria, VA: ASCD.

Jager, W. (2003). Breaking "bad habits": A dynamical perspective on habit formation and change. In L. Hendrickx, W. Jager, & L. Steg (Eds.), *Human decision-making and environmental perception: Understanding and assisting human decision-making in real life settings. Libor Amicourm for Charles Vlek.* Groningen: University of Groningen.

Jensen, E. (1998). *Teaching with the brain in mind.* Alexandria, VA: ASCD.

Jensen, E. (2013). *Engaging students with poverty in mind: Practical strategies for raising achievement.* Alexandria, VA: ASCD.

Johnston, P. (2004). *Choice words: How our language affects children's learning.* Portland, ME: Stenhouse.

Kohlberg, L. (1981). *The philosophy of moral development: Moral stages and the ideas of justice.* New York: Harper & Row.

Kohli, R., & Solorzano, D. G. (2012). Teachers, please learn our names! Racial microaggressions and the K–12 classroom. *Race Ethnicity and Education, 15*(4), 441–462.

Kohn, A. (1993). *Punished by rewards: The trouble with gold stars, incentive plans, A's, praise, and other bribes.* Boston: Houghton Mifflin.

Kraft, T. L., & Pressman, S. D. (2012). Grin and bear it: the influence of manipulated facial expression on the stress response. *Psychological Science, 23*(11), 1372–1378.

Larraway, S., & Scott, K. (2017). *Radically candid criticism.* Randical Candor Podcast, episode 2. Retrieved from https://www.radicalcandor.com/blog/podcast-episode-2/

LeGuin, U. (1968). *A wizard of Earthsea.* New York: Bantam Books.

LeGuin, U. (1970). *The tombs of Atuan.* New York: Bantam Books.

Lepper, M. R., Greene, D., & Nisbett, R. E. (1973). Undermining children's intrinsic interest with extrinsic reward: A test of the "overjustification" hypothesis. *Journal of Personality and Social Psychology, 28*(1), 129–137. Retrieved from http://psycnet.apa.org/record/1974-10497-001

Levitt, S., & Dubner, S. (2005). *Freakonomics: A rogue economist explores the hidden side of everything.* New York: HarperCollins.

Marzano, R. (2003). *What works in schools: Translating research into action.* Alexandria, VA: ASCD.

Medina, J. (2014). *Brain rules: 12 principles for surviving and thriving at work, home, and school.* Seattle, WA: Pear Press.

Navarro, J. (2008). *What every body is saying: An ex-FBI agent's guide to speed-reading people.* New York: HarperCollins.

Newkirk, T. (2017). *Embarrassment: And the emotional underlife of learning.* Portsmouth, NH: Heinemann.

Northeastern University. (2014). Topline report, telephone survey conducted February 3–19: Business elite national poll, 3rd installment of the innovation imperative polling series.

Ouellette, J. A. & Wood, W. (1998). Habits and intention in everyday life: The multiple processes by which past behavior predicts future behavior. *Psychological Bulletin, 124*(1), 54–74.

Pink, D. (2009). *Drive: The surprising truth about what motivates us.* New York: Riverhead Books.

Pink, D. (2012). *To sell is human: The surprising truth about moving others.* New York: Riverhead Books.

Sarcasm [Def. 1]. (n.d.). In *Merriam-Webster online.* Retrieved from https://www.merriam-webster.com/dictionary/sarcasm

Schneider, W., & Shiffrin, R. M. (1977). Controlled and automatic human information processing: I. Detection, search, and attention. *Psychological Review, 84*(1), 1–66.

Thaler, R. H., & Sunstein, C. R. (2008). *Nudge: Improving decisions about health, wealth, and happiness.* New York: Penguin.

Twain, M. (1876). *The adventures of Tom Sawyer.* New York: Grosset & Dunlap, Inc.

Walker, L. J., & Taylor, J. H. (1991). Family interactions and the development of moral reasoning. *Child Development, 62*: 264–283. doi:10.1111/j.1467-8624.1991.tb01530.x

Walsh, J. A., & Sattes, B. D. (2015). *Questioning for classroom discussion: Purposeful speaking, engaged listening, deep thinking.* Alexandria, VA: ASCD.

Willis, J. (2006). *Research-based strategies to ignite student learning: Insights from a neurologist and classroom teacher.* Alexandria, VA: ASCD.

Wormeli, R. (2016). Let's talk about racism in schools. *Educational Leadership, 74*(3), 16–22. Retrieved from http://www.ascd.org/publications/educational-leadership/nov16/vol74/num03/Let's-Talk-about-Racism-in-Schools.aspx

Index

The letter *f* following a page number denotes a figure.

About the Author

 **Mike Anderson** has been an educator for more than 25 years. A classroom school teacher for 15 years, he has also taught preschool and graduate-level university classes. He spent many years as a presenter, consultant, author, and developer for the Northeast Foundation for Children, a nonprofit organization dedicated to helping create safe, joyful, and challenging classrooms and schools. In 2004 Anderson was awarded a national Milken Educator Award, and in 2005 he was a finalist for New Hampshire Teacher of the Year.

Now, as an education consultant, Anderson works with schools in rural, urban, and suburban settings across the United States and beyond. Anderson supports teachers and schools on a wide variety of topics: embedding choice in everyday learning, blending social-emotional and academic teaching, using respectful and effective discipline strategies, staying healthy and balanced as an educator, and many more.

Anderson is the author of many books about great teaching and learning including *The Research-Ready Classroom* (Heinemann, 2006), *The Well-Balanced Teacher* (ASCD, 2010), *The First Six Weeks of School, 2nd Edition* (CRS, 2015), and *Learning to Choose, Choosing to Learn* (ASCD, 2016). His articles have been published in various resources including *Educational Leadership, Language Arts,* Teach.com, and EdCircuit. He has been a guest on Bam! Radio, EduTalk Radio, and the Re:Teaching podcast from the Teacher Learning Sessions. He has also served as an ASCD Whole Child advisor. He also writes frequently on his personal blog through his website.

Anderson lives in Durham, New Hampshire, with his amazing family: Heather, Ethan, and Carly.

To learn more about Anderson and his work, visit his website: www.leadinggreatlearning.com. You can also follow him on Twitter @balancedteacher.

Acknowledgments

I'd like to begin these acknowledgments by recognizing some of the most important thought leaders who have shaped my thinking about language in the classroom (and beyond) over the years. Peter Johnston, Jane Nelson, Alfie Kohn, and Ross Greene—your work has inspired and pushed me, like so many other educators. Your experience with children and your insights into teaching and the language of the classroom have been powerful influences on my evolution as a teacher. I'd also like to especially thank Ruth Charney, Marlynn Clayton, and Paula Denton, whose writing, collegiality, professionalism, coaching, mentorship, and friendship directly shaped who I am and how I think about teaching and language.

There are lots of people who had a substantial impact on the writing of this book. Many teachers in many schools helped me think deeply about how language affects learning, including Barbara Milliken, Chris Hall, Kitri Doherty, Lindsay Lanzer, and Ian Fleischer. I'd like to thank colleagues Kathy Collins, Allison Zmuda, Bena Kallick, Carol Davis, and Kristen Vincent. Your encouragement, support, and many conversations about ideas in this book have made it more complete. My mother, Susan Trask, my wife, Heather Anderson, and my two children, Carly and Ethan, have also been hugely helpful and supportive, enduring (and even enjoying, I hope) the many conversations we've had about this topic. Even our dog, Olive, had a role to play—listening without commenting and offering me chances to walk and clear my head when the writing got tough. There were also several people who read drafts of parts of this manuscript as it was in-process: Shawna Coppola, Andy Dousis, Holly Martin, and my father, Marion Anderson. Your direct and honest feedback was invaluable and much appreciated!

Finally, a special shout-out goes to Genny Ostertag and Liz Wegner, ASCD editors extraordinaire, who helped bring this book to life (and make it a whole lot better in the process). Thanks so much to you and the whole ASCD team!

Related ASCD Resources

At the time of publication, the following resources were available (ASCD stock numbers in parentheses).

Print Products

Learning to Choose, Choosing to Learn: The Key to Student Motivation and Achievement by Mike Anderson (#116015)

The Well-Balanced Teacher: How to Work Smarter and Stay Sane Inside the Classroom and Out by Mike Anderson (#111004)

The Best Class You Never Taught: How Spider Web Discussion Can Turn Students into Learning Leaders by Alexis Wiggins (#117017)

Better Than Carrots or Sticks: Restorative Practices for Positive Classroom Management by Dominique Smith, Douglas Fisher, and Nancy Frey (#116005)

Discipline with Dignity: How to Build Responsibility, Relationships, and Respect in Your Classroom, 4th Edition by Richard L. Curwin, Allen N. Mendler, and Brian D. Mendler (#118018)

The Formative Five: Fostering Grit, Empathy, and Other Success Skills Every Student Needs by Thomas R. Hoerr (#116043)

How to Give Effective Feedback to Your Students, 2nd Edition by Susan M. Brookhart (#116066)

Relationship, Responsibility, and Regulation: Trauma-Invested Practices for Fostering Resilient Learners by Kristin Van Marter Souers with Pete Hall (#119027)

Total Participation Techniques: Making Every Student an Active Learner, 2nd Edition by Pérsida Himmele and William Himmele (#117033)

17,000 Classroom Visits Can't Be Wrong: Strategies That Engage Students, Promote Active Learning, and Boost Achievement by John V. Antonetti and James R. Garver (#115010)

For up-to-date information about ASCD resources, go to www.ascd.org. You can search the complete archives of *Educational Leadership* at www.ascd.org/el.

ASCD myTeachSource®
Download resources from a professional learning platform with hundreds of research-based best practices and tools for your classroom at http://myteachsource.ascd.org/

For more information, send an e-mail to member@ascd.org; call 1-800-933-2723 or 703-578-9600; send a fax to 703-575-5400; or write to Information Services, ASCD, 1703 N. Beauregard St., Alexandria, VA 22311-1714 USA.

THE WHOLE CHILD

The ASCD Whole Child approach is an effort to transition from a focus on narrowly defined academic achievement to one that promotes the long-term development and success of all children. Through this approach, ASCD supports educators, families, community members, and policymakers as they move from a vision about educating the whole child to sustainable, collaborative actions.

What We Say and How We Say It Matter relates to the **engaged, supported,** and **challenged** tenets.
For more about the ASCD Whole Child approach, visit **www.ascd.org/wholechild.**

WHOLE CHILD
TENETS

1 HEALTHY
Each student enters school healthy and learns about and practices a healthy lifestyle.

2 SAFE
Each student learns in an environment that is physically and emotionally safe for students and adults.

3 ENGAGED
Each student is actively engaged in learning and is connected to the school and broader community.

4 SUPPORTED
Each student has access to personalized learning and is supported by qualified, caring adults.

5 CHALLENGED
Each student is challenged academically and prepared for success in college or further study and for employment and participation in a global environment.